D0894281

Bloom's

GUIDES

Maya Angelou's
I Know Why the
Caged Bird Sings
New Edition

Adventures of Huckleberry Finn	The Joy Luck Club
All the Pretty Horses	The Kite Runner
Animal Farm	Lord of the Flies
The Autobiography of Malcolm X	Macbeth
The Awakening	Maggie: A Girl of the Streets
The Bell Jar	The Member of the Wedding
Beloved	The Metamorphosis
Beowulf	Native Son
Black Boy	Night
The Bluest Eye	1984
Brave New World	The Odyssey
The Canterbury Tales	Oedipus Rex
Catch-22	Of Mice and Men
The Catcher in the Rye	One Hundred Years of Solitude
The Chosen	Pride and Prejudice
The Crucible	Ragtime
Cry, the Beloved Country	A Raisin in the Sun
Death of a Salesman	The Red Badge of Courage
Fahrenheit 451	Romeo and Juliet
A Farewell to Arms	The Scarlet Letter
Frankenstein	A Separate Peace
The Glass Menagerie	Slaughterhouse-Five
The Grapes of Wrath	Snow Falling on Cedars
Great Expectations	The Stranger
The Great Gatsby	A Streetcar Named Desire
Hamlet	The Sun Also Rises
The Handmaid's Tale	A Tale of Two Cities
Heart of Darkness	Their Eyes Were Watching God
The House on Mango Street	The Things They Carried
I Know Why the Caged Bird Sings	To Kill a Mockingbird
The Iliad	Uncle Tom's Cabin
Invisible Man	The Waste Land
Jane Eyre	Wuthering Heights

Contents

Introduction

The popularity of *I Know Why the Caged Bird Sings* is proudly based on its achieved pathos: It accomplishes a controlled poignance in representing a portrait of the artist as a young black woman. In the structural background of Maya Angelou's book hover the two prime traditional forms of African-American autobiography, the slave narrative and the African-American version of the church sermon. Each is at once individual and communal, with the two voices sometimes working with each other and sometimes impeding the other's full expression. Angelou, whatever her formal limitations as a poet, is a natural autobiographer who works with considerable skill and with narrative cunning. Her voice interweaves other strands in the African-American oral tradition, but the implicit forms of sermon and slave narrative are ghostly presences in her rhetoric. Angelou brings forward, with a rugged implicitness, a spiritual element vital to all indigenous American religion but original to the African-American paradigm of that religion. The early black Baptists in America spoke of "the little me within the big me," almost the last vestige of the spirituality they had carried with them on the Middle Passage from Africa. Converted to American Baptist Christianity, they brought to the slave owner's faith a kind of gnosis, a radical knowing that "the little me" belonged not to the space and time of this harsh world but to an unfallen realm before the Creation-Fall of the whites. The sermonlike directness of *I Know Why the Caged Bird Sings* is empowered by Angelou's possession of this gnosis, which tells her always that what is best and oldest in her spirit goes back to a lost fullness of being.

Angelou's autobiographical tone is one of profound intimacy and radiates goodwill, even a serenity astonishingly at variance with the terrors and degradations she suffered as a child and as a very young woman. Her voice speaks to something in the

American "little me within the big me," white and black and whatever, that can survive dreadful experiences because the deepest self is beyond experience and cannot be violated, even by such onslaughts as child abuse, rape, and prostitution. Early in this new millennium, where technocracy still renders social compassion obsolete, the prospects for the continued relevance of *I Know Why the Caged Bird Sings* are only enhanced. Despite its secular mode, the book is a spiritual autobiography that addresses the popular imagination of a nation that does not understand its own religion, a Christian gnosis that has little in common with historical European Christianity. We have no history, only biography, and our biography has the single theme: survival of the innermost self. Maya Angelou, incarnating that theme, celebrates the immortality of a deepest self that was not born, and so cannot die, and is always being resurrected.

Biographical Sketch

Maya Angelou is a writer, poet, actress, playwright, civil rights activist, film producer, and director. She lectures throughout the United States and abroad and has published several best-selling books and countless magazine articles. She was born Marguerite Johnson on April 4, 1928, in St. Louis, Missouri, to Bailey and Vivian Baxter Johnson. Her brother Bailey gave her the name Maya. When she was three and a half, her parents divorced and sent her and her brother to Stamps, Arkansas, to live with their paternal grandmother, Annie Henderson.

Angelou describes vividly the desolate journey from California to Arkansas in the autobiography that has since brought her fame, *I Know Why the Caged Bird Sings*, published when she was 41. The book covers her life from childhood and describes the way she was raised in segregated rural Arkansas and St. Louis, Missouri, until the birth of her son when she was 17. Her four subsequent prose books continue her life story, proceeding chronologically. In *Gather Together in My Name* (1974) she depicts her life as a teenage mother, her introduction to drugs and illicit activities, and the hardship of bare economic survival. Her young adult years as a show-business personality provide the content for *Singin' and Swingin' and Gettin' Merry Like Christmas* (1976); her life as a racial and social activist is covered in *The Heart of a Woman* (1981); her African journey from 1962 until 1965 is the topic of *All God's Children Need Traveling Shoes* (1986), and the latest installment of her autobiography, *A Song Flung Up to Heaven* (2002), explores her experiences in the years between 1964 and 1968 after she lived in Ghana.

After graduating from Lafayette Country training school in Arkansas, Maya Angelou, along with her brother, moved to San Francisco, where she attended high school. She received a two-year scholarship to study dance and drama at the California Labor School, but in 1944 she became pregnant and gave birth to a son. In her late teens, she supported herself as a Creole-style cook, nightclub waitress, and streetcar conductor.

In the early 1950s, she married Tosh Angelos. (Her last name is a variation of her then-husband's last name.) Angelos was a Greek sailor whom she met when she worked in a record store in San Francisco.

Sometime during those years, she found her way into a job as a dancer and singer. She had a winning way with audiences, and she performed in the popular West Indian calypso style at the Purple Onion, a cabaret in San Francisco. She also appeared in the role of Ruby in *Porgy and Bess*, a U.S. Department of State–sponsored musical that toured 22 nations. She studied with Martha Graham, and, as she describes in her collection of personal essays, *Wouldn't Take Nothing for My Journey Now* (1993), she had a dancing partnership with Alvin Ailey.

In the late 1950s, after divorcing Tosh, she moved to New York City and became involved in the political and literary scene there. All the while, her career as an actress continued to grow; it reached its high point in 1960 when she played the White Queen in Jean Genet's satirical play *The Blacks*. This was also the most politically active period of her life: She organized a fundraiser called Cabaret for Freedom in support of Martin Luther King Jr. As a result, she was appointed northern coordinator of the Southern Christian Leadership Conference (SCLC), a position she held briefly from 1959 to 1960.

In 1961, she fell in love with a South African dissident lawyer, Vusumzi Make, and moved to Cairo with him. There, she worked as associate editor of *The Arab Observer*, the only English-language news weekly in the Middle East. After her marriage to Make ended, she moved to Ghana, where she worked as assistant administrator of the School of Music and Drama at the University of Ghana.

As she depicts in *All God's Children Need Traveling Shoes*, during her time in Africa she met several people who affected her life and character. One of them was Julian Mayfield, the renowned scholar of W.E.B. Du Bois, and another was black Muslim leader El-Hajj Malik El-Shabazz, known as Malcolm X.

Two horrifying events deeply influenced Maya Angelou on her return to the United States. The first was the assassination of Malcom X on February 21, 1965, and the other was the killing of Martin Luther King in 1968.

In 1971, she published a volume of poetry, *Just Give Me a Cool Drink of Water 'fore I Diiie*, which was nominated for a Pulitzer Prize. Her third marriage, to Paul Du Feu, took place in 1973 (and ended in divorce in 1980). In 1975, President Ford appointed her to the American Revolution Council. Another book of poetry, *And Still I Rise*, was published in 1978. The next collection of poems, *I Shall Not Be Moved*, did not appear till 1990.

In the last three decades, she has written and produced several prize-winning documentaries, including *Afro-Americans in the Arts*, a PBS special for which she received the Golden Eagle, and *Black, Blues, Black*, a 10-part program about the prominent role of African culture in American life. With *Georgia, Georgia*, she became the first black woman to have a screenplay produced. She also wrote the script and musical score for the television version of *I Know Why the Caged Bird Sings*. Along with all of this she has made hundreds of stage and television appearances.

In 1993, at the request of President Bill Clinton, she recited the poem "On the Pulse of Morning" at his inauguration. This was the first time a poet had taken part in an inauguration since Robert Frost spoke at President Kennedy's inauguration. That same year, she published *Wouldn't Take Nothing for My Journey Now*, a collection of essays on lessons in living, which, like most of its predecessors, was a best-seller. Prestigious institutions like Smith College and Mills College have granted her honorary doctorates; reportedly, she now holds 50.

She currently resides in Winston-Salem, North Carolina, where she has a lifetime appointment as the first Reynolds Professor and Chair of American Studies at Wake Forest University.

The Story Behind the Story

Maya Angelou listened to an editor explain that it would be a good idea for her to write her autobiography and to write it as a work of literature. Angelou told him she was too busy. But when he said he believed it might be impossible to do anyway, Angelou jumped right in and said she would do it, showing herself once again as thriving on challenge. She secluded herself and worked assiduously, producing *I Know Why the Caged Bird Sings*, a work of such sensitivity and skill that it earned her a nomination for a National Book Award.

Angelou has told interviewers that it has become her habit when working on a writing project to rent a hotel room and work there, arriving by 6:30 a.m. almost daily. She writes on long yellow tablets until noon or later and then goes home to shower, have a relaxing lunch, and wind down. In the evening, she edits the work. Angelou also has spoken of the challenge and fear of drawing herself back into the past when writing her autobiographies. (*I Know Why the Caged Bird Sings* is her first autobiography in a series of six.) Luckily her memory of certain events is powerful, and in describing or portraying them, she can clearly recall the sights, sounds, and smells of the moment. She believes that her senses developed acutely during the period in her childhood when she was silent.

What appeals to many readers and observers of Angelou's work is her ability to sensitively relay childhood events from a child's perspective and to write with pleasure about the sense-filled experiences that have punctuated her life. While *I Know Why the Caged Bird Sings* has been compared to other works in the black American autobiographical tradition, the work, in its universal reach, moves beyond the techniques and approaches associated with the genre. Black American male autobiographers have written of the search for freedom and education; of the importance of community and the adoption of black pride as a coping mechanism against oppression; of family, nurturing, and the quest for self-sufficiency, personal dignity, and self definition. Angelou and other black women address these concerns and also discuss specifically female issues. For example, throughout Angelou's book, her younger self is concerned with how she looks, and for most of the text she sees herself as ugly for being nonwhite and unfeminine. Yet as the young girl struggles with growing up and becomes more knowledgeable, she develops a positive self-image; she comes to the realization that she can control her own life and to do so must rely on her strong intellect. In this way she also breaks from the slave narratives that describe a journey through chaos, for Angelou realizes she must take the chaos and create her own order.

Like other black female authors, Angelou also writes of the black female's need to cope with men, black and white alike. The greatest tragedy described in her book, for example, is a confrontation not of white against black but of black male adult against black female child, bringing out into the open problems within the black community itself. Some critics have commented that Angelou's job as a writer is tougher than most since she attempts to write for both black and white audiences. Certainly her continued popularity with a diverse audience is a testament to her ably meeting this challenge.

Critics also comment on Angelou's weaving various forms into her work. We know from her autobiography that she was a lover of literature from a young age, appreciating it, looking to it for answers, and finding it a great escape and anchor. Her use of various forms within her own work further exemplifies her delight in the written word. For example, within this autobiography she relates sermons, a ghost story, a children's rhyme, and both secular and religious songs. Her concern with form is also apparent when one examines her methods of structuring consecutive chapters, a chapter itself, or different related sections within the book.

Also prominent in her work is her struggle to find her own way for handling white oppression of blacks. While one critic has remarked that Angelou, for the most part, is an observer of southern prejudice rather than a direct victim of it, Angelou's sensitivity in describing black life remains startlingly vivid. Her deftness radiates in her ability to portray great horrors yet still transcend them. In addition, she shows her talent in her lyrical imagery, self-parody, humor, compassion, portraiture, and storytelling technique, enveloping her reader in a story of poignant realism and hope.

List of Characters

Marguerite Johnson is also called Margaret, Ritie, My, and Maya. The narrator of the book, for the most part she speaks from her childhood perspective. She describes her childhood fears, pains, and needs, all of which are compounded by the additional burden of being black and sent away by divorced parents. She shines because of her love of life, sensitivity, and ability to transcend intense hardship.

Bailey, Maya's brother, is one year older than she. The two have their own world of jokes and secrets and also have an intense bond. Bailey has more courage and charm than Maya, and she sees him as always knowing what to do. He is a strong source of support, innately understanding her hostile feelings about their parents and offering her his advice on how to handle her first white boss and when to tell their mother about her pregnancy.

Annie Henderson, whom the children call Momma, is Maya's grandmother (her father's mother), who raises the children for many years. Maya sees her as the embodiment of great strength. She is stern and determined to rear the children properly and also has the sensitivity and wherewithal to help Maya out of her muteness. She is not formally educated but is full of wisdom, highly religious, hardworking, a great entrepreneur, and quite extraordinary as one of the few black women in Stamps at the time who owned land and a store.

Vivian Baxter, is Maya's mother, beauty personified in Maya's eyes. She is fiercely tough and independent and makes money by running card games. She is the modern city woman living the blues lifestyle. Concerned about providing for her children, she is not so concerned about watching over them.

Bailey Johnson, Sr., Maya's father, is tall and handsome, feigns importance, and wants to appear smooth yet usually speaks in a halting manner. He is insensitive to his children, sending them off to their mother with almost no warning, later laughing when Maya does not get along with his girlfriend, and forcing his daughter to fend for herself in a foreign country while he disappears to get drunk.

Uncle Willie is Maya's uncle and one of Momma's two sons. He lives with Momma, is crippled, and stutters. He believes in Momma's philosophies and harsh child-rearing tactics, threatening to push the children against a hot stove when they miss in reciting their multiplication tables and whipping them with switches after they lose control in church. While blacks are trapped by society's oppression, Uncle Willie is also trapped in a disabled body, and so Maya feels a kinship with him.

Angelou calls **Mrs. Bertha Flowers** her lifeline. Mrs. Flowers is the wealthy, sophisticated, and sensitive woman who draws Maya out of her self-imposed muteness by giving the young girl books. The woman teaches Maya practical lessons about life and also broadens her appreciation of literature, which serves as a great help for Maya throughout the book. Mrs. Flowers is one of the few adults whom Maya admires and thoroughly respects.

The Baxter family is composed of powerful figures, most notably Maya's Grandmother Baxter, who has connections with the police and uses these to trade favors with the St. Louis underground. Her sons are repeatedly described as mean, and we assume they are responsible for Mr. Freeman's death, although this is never explicitly stated.

Mr. Freeman lives with Vivian Baxter when Maya and Bailey are relocated to St. Louis. He is much older than Vivian, and Maya says he is lucky to have her as his girlfriend. Usually quiet, he comes to life around Maya's mother. He rapes Maya and threatens to kill her brother if she tells anyone about it. Mr. Freeman represents the destroyed male and asserts his limited power to prey on children.

Daddy Clidell marries Vivian, and the children live with the new couple the second time they move away from Stamps. Like the Baxters, Daddy Clidell is most comfortable in the underground. He and his con-men friends teach the children how they outwit whites, so the children themselves can never be victimized by such tricks.

Summary and Analysis

"What you looking at me for?
I didn't come to stay . . ."

These lines of poetry begin the **prologue** of *I Know Why the Caged Bird Sings*. They are voiced and repeated in church by the young Maya Angelou, who is intensely embarrassed as she is unable to recall what she must recite next, which provokes giggles from her peers. The lines serve as a foreshadowing of themes and experiences to come: the need to break free of humiliation over one's physical attributes; the struggle of growing up and developing an identity; the combat with racism; the driving desire for a home and its love, security, and unconditional acceptance; and coping mechanisms.

Stuck in a limbo of forgetfulness, Maya hears her rustling taffeta dress and recalls her earlier dream that the dress is magic. As she had watched her grandmother fix it, she "knew" she would look like a movie star in it, "like one of the sweet little white girls who were everybody's dream of what was right with the world." But in the light of Easter morning, she realizes her miracle is illusory. She no longer sees the dress as magical but as an ugly, faded garment discarded by a white woman. Yet she persists in imagining that one day she will snap out of her "black ugly dream" and surprise the world with her long blond hair and light-blue eyes.

Yanked back to her embarrassing reality by the minister's wife, who feeds Maya her final line of poetry, the young girl blurts out the last line and then realizes she has to go to the toilet, quite urgently. She attempts to regain some composure and tiptoes toward the back of the church, only to trip over a child's foot and then feel urine running down her legs. Rushing out into the yard and toward her house crying, she knows she will be punished and teased but laughs anyway, at the "sweet release" and her escape from the "silly church."

The events of the prologue, not occurring in their proper chronological spot in the autobiography, gain much attention, and rightfully so. The young Maya's laughing at an institution traditionally seen as a haven for blacks foreshadows her need to find her own way and not rely on a sanctuary that she views as not providing the proper help. Her embarrassment over her body will remain a key issue throughout the book as well, and her inability to speak will later appear as a self-imposed muteness. The child escapes the church in laughter, just as the author will use humor at other points in the text as relief from the intensity of some of the events described in the book.

Chapter 1 opens with a description of the three-year-old Maya and her four-year-old brother, Bailey, arriving in the small southern town of Stamps, Arkansas, having been shuttled off by their divorcing parents to live with their grandmother. Bailey's name is stated without an explanation of who he is, as if he is so much a part of Maya's life he almost is an extension of herself and therefore needs no introduction (which we will soon find to be the case). The children are haunted by their parents' rejection through most of the book. Not only have they been sent away from their parents and home to a place they hardly know, but they travel by themselves on the long trek from California. Literally, they are labeled like baggage or mail, with tags on their wrists addressed "To Whom It May Concern" and stating their names, addresses, and destination.

The first description upon their arrival is not of their greeting by their grandmother and their uncle, with whom she lives, but of the town's reaction to the children. The imagery reminds us of the children's hunger for love. The town is described as reacting to them "as a real mother embraces a stranger's child. Warmly, but not too familiarly." In short, they still feel unloved. Their literal rejection from their parents' home provokes a longing for a new home, a place that will offer acceptance and love; the loss of home also batters their self worth, for, after all, if their own parents do not love them, what value do they have? In an effort to create some normal childhood experience, the two wayfarers soon start calling their grandmother "Momma."

In this chapter, their grandmother is shown as a successful, smart entrepreneur, owning a general store that is the center of activities in the black part of town. For Maya, it is initially a fun place that becomes one of her favorites. Her grandmother is also shown as religious and industrious. She rises at four o'clock daily, immediately thanks God for not having taken her life overnight, and asks him to "help me to put a bridle on my tongue." Her thanks for not bringing death indicates humble expectations. The request for a bridled tongue mirrors the muteness Maya later experiences and Maya's idea that words can be uncontrollably evil and even cause death.

The store is a gathering place in the morning, when the black workers are full of hope about how much cotton they will pick. Yet at the end of the day, in the "dying" sun, their "supernatural" expectations are ruined by reality—not enough cotton picked, weighted scales, and sacks that will have to be sewn overnight with already sore, stiff fingers. Young Maya is shown here as keenly observant as well as empathic. Later, the author tells us, she would experience "inordinate rage" whenever she saw stereotyped presentations of happy-go-lucky cotton pickers. Such anger is something she will learn to give voice to as she grows in the book. Also notable here is the author's framework of the day that starts hopeful and fades to pain. She uses nature imagery and will show her strength with this technique at other points in the text as well.

A focus on the significant intelligence of the two children (still only five and six years old) both starts and ends **chapter 2**. In the beginning the focus is on math, and at the end it is about literature. Indeed, literature will be a great aid for Maya throughout the book and will be a savior after her traumatic rape at a young age. The chapter opens with Maya and Bailey expertly reciting the multiplication tables. Uncle Willie officiates, pushing them near the burning red potbellied stove if they make too many errors.

Just as the description of their grandmother consumed most of chapter one, Uncle Willie is described in detail in this chapter. This is when we learn that he is crippled—crooked in posture, with a distorted face and one small hand, and unable to walk without a cane. He is made fun of by both children and black men, who struggled to make the barest minimum and were jealous of Uncle Willie, working in a bountiful store with a starched shirt and shining shoes. A rather lengthy description is given of one time when the young Maya watched Uncle Willie pretend that he was not lame. She never learns why at that moment he decided to do so, but again she shows great sympathy for him and others like him, comparing him to a prisoner who is tired of bars and the guilty who tire of blame. Her empathy is so intense that she tells us this is the closest she has ever felt to Uncle Willie, and we recognize that she herself feels helpless and trapped with no possible method of escape. This is just one example of her compassion for others as well as her keen ability to create portraits of people.

Just as in chapter one, where the town's inhabitants are compared to a parent, so, too, here Uncle Willie is compared to a father. Despite the scary punishment he threatens by the stove, Maya sees him as better than her real father. "In fact," she writes, "I would have pretended to be his daughter if he wanted me to. Not only did I not feel any loyalty to my own father, I figure that if I had been Uncle Willie's child I would have received much better treatment." Again we see the primal urge for a parent, even a flawed one. At the same time, we see Maya rejecting her true father, preparing us for her later reactions to him. She has no magical hope for her father or their relationship, no empathy for him like she has for others.

The chapter ends with Maya explaining how she "met and fell in love with William Shakespeare." The word choice almost makes the reader feel Shakespeare is alive. Maya wants us to recognize how alive his writing makes her feel. Yet even at this young age she believes she has to keep this love a secret, since he is a white man and her grandmother would not accept this.

Just as she felt strong empathy with Uncle Willie's plight, and we are not given a clear explanation as to why, here she explains a great attraction to particular lines of Shakespeare and we must discern why. "When in disgrace with fortune and men's eyes" are his words that she says describe a state with which she is most familiar. This fits in with the feeling portrayed in the prologue and that will persist at other points in the book.

The store is Maya's favorite place all the way through age 13. In **chapter 3** she explains her pleasure in opening the front doors like "pulling the ribbon off the unexpected gift," in becoming expert in measuring out just the right amount of dry goods, in experiencing the rhythms of the day among the mackerel, salmon, tobacco, and thread. Many critics comment on Angelou's descriptive skill, and she sensually describes here her love for pineapples and the blissful peace of having dinner at the back of the store. After a day's work, even Uncle Willie's disabilities seem to disappear, and feeding smelly slop to the hogs after dinner doesn't seem to be such a chore.

The pleasures described in this chapter's beginning stand in sharp contrast to the rest of the chapter, which is thick with fear and humiliation. The children overhear Momma being warned by a former sheriff that Uncle Willie should hide because the Ku Klux Klan will be out that night searching for the black man that "messed with" a white woman that day. Angelou provides her reaction years after the event amid the description of the event, which is told from the child's perspective in the real time of her book. Some critics find this technique disturbing, while others believe Angelou manages it quite well. She is sickened by the facts that the former sheriff is proud of himself for providing the warning and that he feels no responsibility for stopping the rampage. Each black man is in danger of losing his life, even one who is seriously crippled. The family immediately sets about emptying the bin that holds potatoes and onions, so that Uncle Willie can squeeze into it. They cover him with layer upon layer of vegetables and hear him moaning throughout the night. Maya is sure he would have been lynched if the "boys" they were warned about had forced Momma to open the store. Very early in the book, then, we see the horrible fear that the evilness of whites causes.

A rather lengthy description of Mr. McElroy, who lives next to the store, opens **chapter 4**. He is notable to the young Maya for being one of the few black men she knows who wears suits. He is an independent black man who owns his land and a large house—"a near anachronism in Stamps." He is a man who keeps to himself but enjoys Uncle Willie's company. Also in his favor, Angelou tells us, is the fact that he never went to church. She and Bailey already must feel the pressure of following the Christian religion in this small town and question its necessity, for they view Mr. McElroy as "courageous" for not giving in to it. Little Maya actually views this as such a formidable act that she excitedly watches him for signs of his next incredible move; he remains a mystery to the child.

Directly following this description of a puzzling, heroic neighbor is the first portrait of Bailey, "the greatest person in my world," according to Maya. Upon reading this glowing testimonial, one is forced to question why it took so long to appear. Why, for example, is a relatively minor next-door neighbor examined first? Perhaps the baffling adult world needs attention first, and a brave adult is the perfect segue to her brother.

At the onset, Maya compares her brother's physical traits to her own. Yet despite her bodily foibles, Bailey still loves her, the young Maya says. This points again to the girl's complete embarrassment over her body, which was made so apparent in the prologue and will persist as a weighty albatross throughout the text. Bailey is so wonderful for always taking revenge when others make fun of his sister's looks. Again, this example focuses on her appearance, and, even worse, the young girl cites her own elder relatives as being responsible for the rude comments. Bailey's ability to get back at them shows his cunning and serves as one of the earliest examples in the book of children being aware they are smarter, more sensitive, and more virtuous than the adults. Bailey is outrageous and exacting and has boundless energy. Yet seldom is he punished, since he is the pride of the family, which the young girl accepts without feeling weakened or in competition. He is so incredible to the lonely Maya that she calls him her "unshakable God."

The chapter switches to covering traditions in the town related to food. At least twice a year Maya and Bailey go into town to buy real meat, with Bailey, of course, being the one to carry the money. Fellow black inhabitants are all greeted along the way, and friends are even briefly visited—there is a notably different atmosphere than the one confronting them on the white side of town. Segregation keeps the children from seeing many white people, which makes Maya never believe that "whites are really real." She does know they must be dreaded, as they live their "alien unlife."

An explanation of Momma's two key commandments— "Thou shall not be dirty" and "Thou shall not be impudent"— opens **chapter 5**. Maya and her brother must be clean, even if it requires washing outside on the bitterest nights. Also, they must treat their elders with the utmost respect. Everyone Maya knows follows these rules, except for "powhitetrash children," whom Maya describes as living on Momma's land but still treating her Uncle Willie and Momma not only in the most disrespectful manner but as if they were mere servants. These descriptions smoothly set up the reader for the climactic event of the chapter—Momma's confrontation with young white girls who mock her in an attempt to get her to lose control. Maya describes it as "the most painful and confusing experience I had ever had with my grandmother."

Momma poses a formidable opponent. She sees the girls coming up the street and decides not to turn away but to face them, the whole time remaining steady and singing to herself. The girls mimic and tease and culminate their attempts to unsettle Momma by having one girl wearing a dress but no underwear stand on her head. As the young girl's skirt falls over her face, Momma continues to hum, in complete control as her "apron strings trembled."

Before the girls arrive, Momma has made Maya go inside, and the young granddaughter observes the whole shameful scene through the screen door, wishing Momma were inside with her or had let Maya face the girls on her own. Maya wishes she could shoot the girls, scream, or throw black pepper, or even lye, on them. Yet in the same sentence containing these desires, she remarks, "but I knew I was as clearly imprisoned behind the scene as the actors outside were confined to their roles." She recognizes the deranged societal machine at work. Yet while Maya has burst into tears, Momma sings "Glory, glory, hallelujah," triumphant, albeit within society's very sick rules. This is an example of Angelou's writing fitting into the narrative slave tradition, as many critics have commented. The evil, prejudiced system is a part of everyday life, and the author works to find ways to fight it, just as the slave writers did.

In **chapter 6**, a sharp portrait is given of Reverend Howard Thomas, a preacher who would visit their Christian Methodist Episcopal Church in Stamps every three months and stay at Momma's house the night before his Sunday sermon. Maya and Bailey despised him, not only because he was ugly and fat but because he never remembered their names, always ate the best chicken parts at their Sunday meal, and droned on and on with his blessing until the food was quite cold.

The family heads off to church on one Sunday when Reverend Thomas is to preach, and in able storyteller fashion, Angelou precedes the description of the event with her recollection of another church occurrence. On that remembered day, one churchgoer, Sister Monroe, became so full of the spirit that she ran up to their usual preacher on the pulpit, yelling, "Preach it," and inspiring two others to do the same. This resulted in a scuffle, with the reverend and two others down on the altar floor. For weeks after, all Bailey had to do was say, "Preach it," and the two children would break into laughter.

This recollection prepares the reader for what could happen on this particular hot day in church, which Angelou returns to describing. She tells us that Momma sits directly in view of the two children, so she can cast them appropriately stern looks as needed to keep them behaving. When Maya looks over to her on this day, though, Momma's watchful eye is on Sister Monroe instead of the children. Sister Monroe's voice quickly becomes loud during the service. A few children try to stifle giggles, and Bailey nudges his sister, saying, "Preach it." While two men try to hold Sister Monroe to prevent another embarrassment, she will not be restrained and rushes once again to the pulpit.

Reverend Thomas, who has heard the story of her previous escapade, immediately starts off the pulpit from the side opposite her, continuing his preaching. While many other churchgoers are following Sister Monroe, she does catch up with the reverend and hits him on the back of the head with her purse—twice—causing his false teeth to catapult from his mouth and to the floor just next to Maya's shoe. By this time, Maya is consciously holding back laughter, but she cannot manage once she hears laughing snorts emanating from her brother. Reminiscent of the experience related in the prologue, Maya again has lost control in church, but this time she and her brother are in it together. They laugh with complete abandon, slipping off the bench, screaming, and kicking and laughing even louder when they look at each other.

Momma yells to them; Uncle Willie, who is closest, threatens to whip them, and they end up in the parsonage next door being beaten by Uncle Willie. He persists, and they are saved not when a sympathetic churchgoer forces him to stop but when the minister's wife asks him to stop because their cries are interrupting what is left of the service. While at least one critic has written about Momma's religion as one of the strongest influences on Maya's life, apparently it is not necessarily a strong positive influence when in the confines of the church. Instead it is absurdist, not necessarily because of what the church stands for but because the church is composed of people with comical foibles. As will occur at other points in the book, the children see the insanity of the very adults whom they are supposed to respect.

Many critics also have spoken of Angelou's keen skill with humor, working it through her book at key points and using it as a saving grace from the tragedy strewn throughout the work. Angelou uses hope in a similar way, although the hope that Momma has is strongly based on her traditional religious perspective, while Maya's seems to come from another source. Whatever their sources, both humor and hope make the young girl's life livable, when at times it is so very bad. They serve as a wonderful testament to Angelou as well as to the human spirit.

In the very brief **chapter 7**, we are given more insight into Momma, who was married three times but whose spouses remain a mystery to the children. They hear from others in the town that Momma was pretty when she was young, but all that Maya can see in her is her strength. Momma intends to teach Maya and Bailey life's lessons as she and all the blacks before her had learned them. The only lesson stated here is her perspective on how to deal with whites. She believed that one risked one's life if one spoke to a white person and that even in their absence they should not be spoken of harshly. She saw this approach not as cowardly, but realistic.

The attempt to understand whites continues in the beginning of **chapter 8**. While whites are, for the most part, separate from blacks, the children develop what Angelou calls a "fear-admiration-contempt" for the whites' cars, houses, children, and women. Maya cannot understand how they can spend money so lavishly. While her grandmother had more money than the poor whites and owned land and houses, she still taught the children to waste nothing. "Of course, I knew God was white too, but no one could have made me believe he was prejudiced," Maya rationalizes. Her child's logic assumes that if the whites are rich, powerful, and beautiful, God must be one of them. Again, she is on the outside.

Once the Depression hits the small town, though, the ability to even consider wasting anything completely vanishes. Momma uses her businesswoman's acumen to keep her poor customers still coming to her store even though many are now struggling financially. Starkly contrasted to this intense trouble is the life Maya hears her parents are living "in a heaven called California, where we were told they could have all the oranges they could eat. And the sun shone all the time. I was sure that wasn't so. I couldn't believe that our mother would laugh and eat oranges in the sunshine without her children." Maya had believed her parents were dead until one Christmas when the parents sent toys for her and Bailey. The children reacted to the presents by going out in the cold and crying. Now that their parents must be alive, Maya is consumed with wondering why they had sent their own children away, figuring that she and Bailey must have done something terribly wrong.

Bailey tells Maya that if the toys really did come from their parents, it might mean that they would be coming to take the children back. Maybe their parents had finally forgiven them for whatever they had done. Both children destroy the doll that was sent but save the tea set, so they will have it when their parents appear. The doll is described in a straightforward way as having blond hair and blue eyes—the exact traits that we learned in the prologue that Maya wishes she had and is so embarrassed to not have. This is only one of the first great pains the parents will cause their children.

Chapter 9 occurs one year later on the day their father appears, just as Bailey anticipated, with seemingly no warning. All of their imaginings of him must now be thrown aside. He is big and "blindingly handsome." Maya is so proud of him and knows he must be rich "and maybe had a castle out in California." But she also has fears that maybe he is not her real father and that she is just an orphan the family had picked up to keep Bailey company. For three weeks their father is the center of attention at the store as people come to see him, and then he announces that he must go back to California. Maya is relieved until she learns that he is taking her and Bailey with him.

Maya panics and does not know if she should really go. But she ends up squeezed in the back of the car, emotionally and physically uncomfortable. Bailey and their father make jokes in the front, and she is disturbed to realize that Bailey is trying to butter him up. The children then receive their next monumental shock: They are not going to California but to St. Louis to meet their mother. Maya is immediately terrified, fearful that her mother might laugh at them the way their father has or that her mother might have other children living with her now. Maya says she wants to go back to Stamps, cries, and asks Bailey in pig Latin if he thinks that this is their real father or a kidnapper.

St. Louis is described as hot, dirty, and rather ominous. Maya is "struck dumb" by her mother's beauty, which "literally assailed me." Mother wears lipstick, the first sign that this is a very different woman from their grandmother, who had said wearing lipstick was a sin. Mother has an enormous smile, and Maya surmises that she had sent them away because she was too beautiful to have children. Bailey is immediately in love with her and has forgotten her rejection of them. Their father leaves the children in St. Louis after a few days, and Maya remarks that it hardly mattered either way, since both he and her mother are strangers to her.

This chapter again focuses on physical description. Angelou, the master portrait artist, chooses to focus on surface characteristics—not only because this is always a large part of one's first impression of a person but also because it indicates the child's obsession with her own physicality and how it fits in with the world. Also, it seems fitting that little is said about the father's personality, even after the children have been with him for weeks, because he is, in fact, a man overly concerned with the surface. The quotes showing Maya's immediate reaction to her mother also serve as a foreshadowing of terrible events yet to occur because of their living with their mother.

A more thorough taste of St. Louis and Mother's Baxter family is given to the reader in **chapter 10**. The black section of St. Louis is replete with gambling and other illegal activities, and those who partake of these practices are frequenters of Grandmother Baxter's house, where the children live for their first six months in St. Louis. Grandmother Baxter is a powerful figure in the community because of her six mean offspring and her ability to pull strings with the police. An entourage of crooks request her help and in return provide her with favors. She has a strong marriage with her husband, who lives for his family and actually encourages his grown sons to fight. Mother is the only outgoing sibling, but Maya is fascinated by the men's meanness.

In their new school, Maya and Bailey are shocked that their fellow classmates know so little. The teachers recognize the abilities of the two new children and move them ahead a grade so as not to intimidate their peers. In the year that they attend this school, Maya recalls learning almost nothing. The teachers are more formal, cold, and condescending than they had been in Stamps. The children learn to no longer use the phrase "Yes ma'am" and are told to answer with just "Yes." This is only one example of how the teachings of their grandmother in Arkansas no longer apply in the world of St. Louis.

The children's lives are remarkably different. Instead of being under the steady watchfulness of their Stamps grandmother, here in St. Louis they seldom even see their mother at home. Occasionally she has them meet her in a dark tavern after school, where they watch her dance and sing the blues. The children learn the time step and are required to show their skill at the bar; it is a far cry from the days of reciting the times tables by the potbellied stove, yet Maya approaches the task with the same dedication.

After six months, the children move in with their mother and have to adjust yet again. While it is never spoken of, Maya constantly feels the threat that Mother could return them to Stamps if they are disobedient or too troublesome. As a result, the young girl alters her demeanor, making no move without extreme care. Also in this chapter, the reader gains a brief glimpse of Mother's boyfriend, Mr. Freeman, who lives with her. Maya sees him as notably older than her mother and lucky to have her.

Maya tells us in **chapter 11** that St. Louis is a foreign country that she will never get used to. She does not view it as home. "I carried the same shield that I had used in Stamps: 'I didn't come to stay,'" Angelou writes. This is a flashback to the prologue, where she had to recite these exact words in church. The lines, then, are not just words adults forced her to memorize but words that she views as applicable to her life. Yet whereas the idea of the first line of poetry, which deals with identity and not fitting in, has been recurring throughout the first 10 chapters, the relevance of the second line never has been pointedly stated in the book until now. While we have recognized Maya's longing for being accepted and loved in a stable home, this is the first statement telling us that all along she has kept herself from letting her defenses down, from ever allowing herself to believe she really could be home. While the defense helps ease her pain, her desire for a home and love will persist throughout the book and manifest itself in various ways. For example, both Maya and Bailey develop "afflictions." Bailey stutters, and Maya has terrifying nightmares, causing her mother to sometimes bring the girl into bed with her and Mr. Freeman.

One morning Mother has gotten up early, leaving Maya alone in the bed with Mr. Freeman. He involves the young girl in his masturbation, and she is confused yet feels very comforted when he holds her afterwards. So intense are her needs that she says, "I feel at home," the very feeling she previously has prevented herself from having. It is a poignant scene. "From the way he was holding me," Angelou writes, "I knew he'd never let me go or let anything bad ever happen to me. This was probably my real father and we had found each other at last."

But Mr. Freeman threatens Maya, saying that if she ever tells anyone what happened that morning he will kill Bailey. The young girl is stunned and confused. Angelou writes that she did not dislike Mr. Freeman at this point but "simply didn't understand him." For a brief few weeks, Maya actually wishes he would hold her again. Unwittingly she climbs into his lap, provoking his ejaculation, after which he stops speaking to her for months. She feels lonely and rejected but soon forgets about him and loses herself in books and comic strips. Since Bailey is more distanced from her, the books pose a fantastic escape, and she spends most of her Saturdays at the library, completely undisturbed.

While Maya nearly has forgotten about the sexual incidents with Mr. Freeman, in **chapter 12** the reader learns that these encounters are not over. This time is different, though. As soon as Maya realizes Mr. Freeman's intentions, she backs away and says no to him, despite the fact that she had liked it when he held her before. This time is also worse, because Mr. Freeman rapes the eight-year-old girl, and she faints.

Mr. Freeman tells Maya again that she must not tell anyone what has happened. She promises not to and says she must go lie down. Instead, he hands her the soggy underwear that he has rinsed out and sends her off to the library. The child is half delirious, walking down the street and feeling like her hips are coming out of their sockets, and so she returns home and goes to bed. Her mother and Bailey are concerned and assume she is sick, since so many children then have the measles. When they leave Maya's room, Mr. Freeman looms over the girl and again threatens her to not tell anyone. Through the night Maya keeps waking to hear her mother and Mr. Freeman arguing, and she hopes he will not hurt Mother too.

In the morning, Mother tells Maya that Mr. Freeman has moved out, and the young girl wonders whether that means it is safe to tell what really happened to her. She wonders whether Bailey will still love her. She fears she is dying and asks Bailey to take her away to California or France or Chicago. Since Maya has sweated so much, Mother says they must change the sheets, and this is when they find Maya's stained underwear, which she has hidden under the mattress.

Chapter 13 opens with Maya in the hospital and Bailey asking her who hurt her. She explains that she must keep this a secret, since the man will kill Bailey. But when her brother says that he will not let that happen, she, in her child-like innocence, believes him and tells him. He breaks into tears, and Maya starts to cry as well.

Mr. Freeman is arrested, and shortly thereafter Maya testifies against him in an overcrowded courtroom, filled with, among others, Grandmother's thuglike acquaintances. Afraid as the lawyer tries to trip her up, Maya swears to herself that she hears people in the courtroom laughing at her. Then she stiffens in even greater fear when the lawyer asks her whether Mr. Freeman had ever touched her before the day of the supposed rape. If she tells the truth, she believes her uncles will kill her, Grandmother Baxter will stop speaking to her, Mother will be so disappointed, and, worst of all, Bailey will find out that she has kept big secrets from him.

Feeling very pressured, the young Maya lies and says that Mr. Freeman had never touched her before. Immediately upon speaking the words, she feels a lump in her throat as though she cannot breathe. Mr. Freeman is found guilty and sentenced to prison, yet he manages to get released the very same day.

At home later that day, Maya fears she is really in trouble when a policeman comes to the door. She and Bailey hear the man tell their grandmother that Mr. Freeman has been killed. "Poor man," Grandmother whispers, and then she asks whether they know who killed him. She plays the sympathetic role with the policeman, yet the reader, who has already heard about the ruthlessness of the Baxter clan, can guess what has happened.

Angelou draws us immediately back into Maya's thoughts. The young girl is shocked, assuming that because she has lied, she is responsible for Mr. Freeman's death. She believes that she will never go to heaven. "Even Christ himself turned His back on Satan. Wouldn't He turn His back on me?" she asks herself. "I could feel the evilness flowing through my body and waiting, pent up, to rush off my tongue if I tried to open my mouth. I clamped my teeth shut, I'd hold it in." The young Maya is horrified and cannot even talk to Bailey about it. He, too, is terrified.

Maya decides right then not to speak again, except to Bailey, for she is convinced that if she does speak, another person may die. This reaction is at first accepted by the family, but when the doctor declares the child healed, everyone expects her to return to her previous self. When she does not, she is called impudent and sullen and then is punished. Yet none of this brings Maya back, and so the occurrence that the children had dreaded from the moment they arrived takes place: They are sent back to Arkansas. With her defensive shield up, Angelou claims she does not care about being sent away. She does care very much, however, that her best buddy Bailey is completely distraught over leaving.

"The barrenness of Stamps was exactly what I wanted . . . ," Angelou writes in **chapter 14**. "Into this cocoon I crept." She appreciates the fact that nothing happens in Stamps and that she no longer has to cope with the freewheeling St. Louis. The two children now have celebrity status in Stamps. After all, they had been whisked away in a big, shiny car by a well-spoken father with a "big-city accent" to a glamorous place and have returned to tell about it. Momma is so proud of them she does not immediately make them responsible for chores. Bailey sops up the limelight, telling tall tales of the height of skyscrapers in St. Louis, the bounty of their watermelons, and the monstrous depth of their snow. Maya remains mute, not only not emitting sound herself but struggling with letting sounds in as well. Her senses are dulled, and she worries about her sanity. The people of Stamps accept her silence as part of her "tender-hearted" nature, viewing her as overly sensitive and "in delicate health."

Yet upon reading the events in **chapter 15**, the reader realizes that Momma knows Maya cannot stay mute forever and that something should be done to help her. At the opening of the chapter, Maya tells us that she remains quiet for nearly a year but then becomes acquainted with a woman "who threw me my first life line." The woman is Mrs. Bertha Flowers, one of the few aristocratic blacks in their town. Before we even find out about how Maya meets this woman, Angelou writes that Mrs. Flowers "was one of the few gentlewomen I have ever known, and has remained throughout my life the measure of what a human can be."

While Mrs. Flowers is so different from Momma, the two have an intimacy that Maya does not understand. Maya is embarrassed when she hears Momma use improper English when speaking to the beautiful, refined woman. The young girl is even more embarrassed when Mrs. Flowers compliments Momma on her sewing. In response, Momma insists on lifting Maya's dress over her head to show the woman that even the stitches on the inside are nearly perfect. Mrs. Flowers realizes Maya's dismay and politely tries to keep Momma from pulling the dress over the young girl's head, yet another sign of the woman's sensitivity and grace.

Maya is told to walk home with Mrs. Flowers and carry her groceries. En route Mrs. Flowers says she knows that Maya's written schoolwork is very good but that the teachers have trouble getting her to talk in class. She says that no one will make her talk but explains that language is what separates man from the lower animals, which gets Maya thinking. Mrs. Flowers also says that she knows the young girl reads a lot but that it is necessary for the human voice to infuse the written word with deeper meaning. Maya readily soaks this in as well.

Maya is enchanted by the woman's home and the fact that she has made lemonade and cookies just for Maya and even gives her extras to bring home for her brother. She listens as Mrs. Flowers explains that even though some people have not been fortunate enough to have a formal education, the young girl must realize that some of them are even more intelligent than college professors. Apparently the woman has sensed Maya's embarrassment over her own grandmother. Mrs. Flowers reads aloud to Maya and gives her books to take home, telling her to pick a poem to memorize, so she can recite it at their next visit.

The young girl runs home in a rush of excitement. "I was liked, and what a difference it made. I was respected not as Mrs. Henderson's grandchild or Bailey's sister but for just being Marguerite Johnson," Angelou writes. She is thrilled to have had Mrs. Flowers read to her from her favorite book and make cookies just for her. The identity issues that have posed a major problem for the girl throughout the book so far finally are being chipped away.

Momma hits Maya with a switch upon her return from her visit with Mrs. Flowers because she misunderstands something the girl says, interpreting it as a curse. The incident points out how different the world of Mrs. Flowers is from Momma's world. But Momma is at least partially responsible for the meeting of Maya and Mrs. Flowers, and the fact that she wants her grandchildren to grow up properly shows the possibility for a valuable mixing of the two very different worlds. Once again, Angelou proves herself the able designer of her tale, as many critics note, setting up striking contrasts at both the start and end of the chapter.

The rich life of Mrs. Flowers also contrasts with that of an upper-class white woman, Mrs. Viola Cullinan, with whom Maya gets a job in **chapter 16**, as part of her education about life's "finer touches." Maya is taught by Miss Glory, Mrs. Cullinan's cook, whose slave ancestors had also worked for the rich woman's family. Miss Glory is very patient with Maya, and Maya is fascinated with the novelty of the many pieces of silverware, special dishes and glasses for specific purposes, and many pieces that she had never known existed. She feels sorry for the plump Mrs. Cullinan when she finds out that her husband has had two children with a black woman.

Yet the pity quickly wears away when Mrs. Cullinan's friend suggests she call Maya "Mary," since it is shorter than her full name of Margaret. The next day Mrs. Cullinan does, in fact, take the suggestion and use the name Mary. She explains to

Glory that this name is shorter and will be what she uses from now on. Maya is furious and feels no better when Glory tries to calm her by telling her that Mrs. Cullinan shortened her name too and that it actually worked out quite well.

When Maya later discusses the effrontery with Bailey, he devises the perfect stratagem that will not only bring revenge but get Maya out of ever having to go back to Mrs. Cullinan's. The next day Maya carries out the plan. She purposefully drops an empty serving tray. When Mrs. Cullinan yells "Mary!" Maya drops the woman's favorite casserole piece and two of her favorite green glass cups. Mrs. Cullinan falls on the floor, and she begins to cry. When her friend asks her whether "Mary" did this, Mrs. Cullinan yells back, "Her name's Margaret, god-damn it, her name's Margaret!" as she throws a broken piece of plate at Maya. Mrs. Cullinan has learned her lesson, and this is the first time in the book that Maya successfully fights for her dignity. It is notable that the confrontation is caused by the woman's not accepting Maya's name or identity, since developing an identity is one of the strongest concerns in the book.

Yet another of the key concerns in the book is that fear is common not only for the two children but for blacks in general. **Chapter 17** opens on a seemingly normal Saturday morning, Maya's favorite day of the week, even though it is filled with a lengthy list of chores. Yet the typical day becomes haunting when Bailey does not return from the movies at his usual time and it becomes darker and darker as the family waits for him. Maya feels she has the most to lose if he is found dead, for he is all she has.

Angelou describes the night as "enemy territory" as she and Momma walk with a flashlight to meet Bailey. "The Bluebeards and tigers and Rippers could eat him up before he could scream for help," we are told by the young Maya. Finally Bailey's figure is seen ahead in the dark. When Maya and Momma reach him, he provides no explanation of where he has been and even pushes Maya away as if she is a stranger. She is completely confused and frightened by his lack of response and seemingly overwhelming look of sadness. Upon their return home, Bailey is whipped by Uncle Willie for causing the family grief, and all the while the boy makes no response.

For days Bailey is in his own world. His eyes are vacant; he doesn't speak. Finally he tells Maya that he saw their mother. He explains that he did not really see her but saw a white actress who looked exactly like her on the movie screen. He had stayed so late at the theater the week before because he had to watch the film again. Maya understands why he could not talk to Momma or Uncle Willie about it. "She was never mentioned to anyone because we simply didn't have enough of her to share," Angelou writes, referring to their mother. Months later there is another movie in town featuring the same actress, and this time Maya goes with her brother to see it. It makes her very happy, but it disturbs Bailey deeply again.

Chapter 18 opens at the end of a weekday at the store, with Maya giving an account of the exhausted field workers. "I thought them all hateful to have allowed themselves to be worked like oxen, and even more shameful to try to pretend that things were not as bad as they were," the young Maya thinks, again disgusted not so much with the black plight as with the black response to it. One worker tells Momma he is going to the revival meeting, and Maya wonders whether her race is full of masochists since the man rightfully should be going home to collapse into bed.

Angelou takes us to the revival meeting, which the young girl finds shocking for being in a tent rather than in a church and for bringing together the very different people from all of the surrounding churches. The minister's sermon is about charity, but more importantly, about what charity is not. It is not about giving someone a job and then expecting the person to bend down in thanks, he says. Nor is it about paying someone for work and then insisting that the worker call the employer "master," nor about asking that he humble and belittle himself. In short, charity is not about the things that the white people do. The assembled have renewed faith from participating in the service; they know that the white people will get what they deserve and that they themselves must manage through the troubles of this world but will live in a blissful eternity. It is unfortunate, though, that so soon after they leave the tent the reality of the current world floods back in.

A temporary victory also occurs in **chapter 19** as the black townspeople squeeze into the store to hear the Joe Louis fight on the radio. As we listen to the radio announcer and the blacks in the store, we never hear the name of the person Louis is fighting but do know what is most important—that he is fighting a white man. With every serious blow that Louis takes, we are told, the entire black race suffers as well. The store is tense until the fight ends and Louis wins and keeps his heavyweight champion title. There is a great celebration in the store, complete with Cokes and candy bars, and there is even alcohol out back. Similar to what occurs in the previous chapter, though, this is only a fleeting victory. People who live far from the store stay in town that night because it is not safe "for a Black man and his family to be caught on a lonely country road on a night when Joe Louis had proved we were the strongest people in the world."

A more pleasant event is the summer picnic and fish fry in **chapter 20**. Even here, though, Maya wishes she had a book to read and finds a quiet spot off by herself. Her sanctuary is invaded by another young girl, Louise Kendricks, who is also 10 years old and whom Maya had always believed to be the prettiest female in Stamps after Mrs. Flowers. The two girls are of similar spirit; they play creative games away from the others, giggle and laugh uproariously, and become true friends.

In the same chapter, Angelou writes about receiving a request that she become a fellow classmate's valentine, to which she has mixed reactions. The young girl wonders if it could be a joke or whether the classmate has evil intentions. She becomes more disturbed when Louise explains that the writer of the valentine wants her to be "his love." Maya rips the message in half, and each girl shreds her part into little pieces and lets them escape in the wind.

Adults are shown to be foolish, insensitive, and unaware of children's feelings in this chapter and others in the book. In this instance, Maya's teacher reads out loud some valentines and a note from Maya's admirer. Maya realizes from the sincerity of the note that perhaps it was a mistake to have torn up the first one. She decides to say something extra nice to the boy who wrote it when he comes in the store, yet she is continually tongue-tied and eventually he stops noticing her.

Chapter 21 turns to Bailey's sexual maturation, quite a contrast from Maya's experience in the previous chapter. His concern is with the physical aspects, and he rather innocently lures girls into a tent in the backyard. After a few months of this, he meets a sexually advanced girl who is older than he and to whom he becomes most attached. Yet all is not well with this relationship, for whereas before the young girl would do chores around the store, now she seldom does. Also, Bailey is taking items from the store, some of the most expensive ones, to satiate her.

Just as Bailey's personality had changed when he first met the girl, when she disappears, he is severely affected as well. He loses interest in life and becomes uncommunicative. The children find out later that the girl had run away with a railroad porter but that she had considered Bailey her only friend in Stamps. The events in the two successive chapters clearly point out the siblings' differing reactions to relationships and members of the opposite sex, just as before these chapters we see their disparate reactions to the movie star who looks like their mother. Whereas Bailey has always been the strong one, in both of these instances Maya appears stronger, although in the instance of the valentine, she initially had rejected its sender to avoid any possible pain. For both children, though at different points, silence serves as a coping mechanism.

In chapter 22 Maya is confronted with another fact of life—death. Angelou displays the still-young Maya's reaction to death as initially based on fear, a belief in ghosts, and her active imagination, which has been fed by an array of literature. On a stormy night when a tornado is threatening, she is reading *Jane Eyre* as Momma cooks and Bailey and Uncle Willie also are reading. She is the first to hear a rattle at the door, and Bailey lets in their neighbor George Taylor, whose wife has died six months ago. Maya fixates on his compelling watery eyes. He proceeds to tell the family that his wife spoke to him just the night before and told him she wanted some children. When he says he will tell them exactly what happened, Maya cringes in fearful anticipation of hearing a real ghost story.

Angelou delays the telling of the ghost story and interjects Maya's memory of Mrs. Taylor's funeral, the first one she had ever attended. In listening to the preacher and observing the other funeral attendees, she had come to the grown-up realization that death will come even to her. With this as a backdrop, the young Maya fearfully watches and listens to Mr. Taylor's nightmare. He assures the family that it was not a dream but that it truly happened. He relates how an angel appeared to him, laughing, and spoke in the voice of his wife, telling him she wanted to have children. When they ask him again if it could have been a dream, he is adamant that this really happened. By then Maya is shaking and believes everyone else in the room is as well. Yet Momma responds calmly when Mr. Taylor asks her what this event means, and she gives her realistic, non-supernatural interpretation. Within minutes the room is relieved of the "intoxication of doom" and returns to normal, similar to what happens after other intense experiences described in previous chapters.

Trembling children are again described in **chapter 23**, but at this point the trembling is in anticipation of a great, exciting event. Some of the largest classes are graduating from both the elementary school and high school in Stamps, and Maya will be one of the eighth-grade graduates. She has been a top student and will receive special note at the ceremony. In the meantime, she is the center of attention at home and in the store. Her grandmother is working diligently on making her dress, and it is nothing like the dress that she had been so humiliated to wear in the prologue. In fact, this dress and Maya's emotions are very different from what they had been on that day and on most other days described so far in the book. Now her dress is beautiful and makes her look like a sunbeam. "I was going to be lovely," Angelou writes. Even her hair, which she has complained about so many times before, which she had wished was a golden blond, is now cooperative and pleasing.

Indeed, there is a momentous shift in the chapter. The girl who had been mute, who had thrown up shields in an attempt to prevent herself from emotional harm, is transformed. "The faded beige of former times had been replaced with strong and sure colors," Angelou writes. She has found new happiness; she smiles so much her jaw hurts; she "trammeled memories of slights and insults. . . . Lost years were pounded to mud and then to dust." Finally, the young girl has hope.

In light of this, it appears quite unfortunate when Maya's graduation ceremony starts with foreboding. The program is changed to accommodate a speaker who is on a tight schedule. He is a white man who lets them know of all the improvements the white school would be receiving. Also, he assures them that he has explained to powerful people that great athletes have come out of their black school. If elected, he will ensure that their school becomes the only black school in that part of Arkansas with a paved playing field. Possibly they could also get new equipment for their home economics and wood-shop classes.

As the young children listen, their heads drop in shame and disappointment. Maya says the day is ruined. She is again disgusted at having no control over her life because of her blackness. She hardly can stomach the rest of the ceremony. But then a hush falls on the room, and the top boy in her class, usually quiet and conservative, leads the class in singing the song that had become known as the Negro national anthem. Parents join in, and the small children who had performed earlier are led back onstage to sing as well. While at other points in the book Maya has remained repulsed by the black situation and blacks' seemingly foolish hope, here there is a great difference. Now she feels a great communal hope and is proud to be black. Unlike other chapters, in which hope disappeared at their ends, here Angelou sustains immense optimism. The transcendence that occurs despite adversity and that is described here and at other points in the work are part of the book's great strength and part of what makes Angelou herself quite astounding.

There is another clash between black and white in **chapter 24**, and again it differs from most of those that have occurred previously. Now Maya has an unbearable toothache, and Momma is ready to fight convention by taking her to see the white dentist in town. He never treats blacks, but Momma believes that, since she had lent him money when he was desperate, he owes her a favor. At the dentist's back door, Momma and Maya have to wait for more than an hour before he will talk to them. Momma is determined to get Maya treatment, yet the doctor will not give in. Finally, he makes a horrid comment about blacks and closes the door on Momma and Maya.

But Momma, not ready to give in, makes Maya wait outside as she goes in after the dentist. Angelou gives us Maya's imaginative view of what is taking place. As long as she is given the chance to dream, the young girl dreams big, picturing Momma ordering the dentist out of town by sundown and to never practice dentistry again, as he shakes and cries, helpless before her. On Momma's way out, Maya imagines, she turns the dentist's nurse into a sack of chicken feed. This fantastical victory shows that imagination and storytelling can create escapes from prejudice. The fantasy also hints, according to one critic, that imagination and storytelling can be forms of resisting racism as well.

When Momma does actually come out, she takes Maya on a Greyhound bus to the black dentist. Later we learn the true story of what happened at the white dentist's office. Momma had pushed the dentist enough to get him to give her 10 dollars for the bus fare. She had not gotten exactly what she had wanted, but she certainly had not lost either. Even Momma cannot always follow her own advice about steering clear of whites. Maya and the reader get an even greater perspective on Momma's strength and tenacity.

While chapter 24 ends with Momma and Uncle Willie laughing over her conquest at the dentist's, **chapter 25** is solemn. Momma announces that she will take the children back to California. Angelou explains that no matter what reason Momma would have given as to why she was planning the trip, the main reason was something that had happened to Bailey.

After this ominous introduction, Angelou proceeds to tell us what that was.

Bailey had arrived home one night shaking and unable to speak. This reminds the reader of the earlier chapter when Bailey had been stunned by the movie star that looked like his mother. There, too, the young Maya had been extremely frightened, and the reader wonders if here, too, her anticipatory fear is greater than what the situation may deserve. When Bailey finally talks, he tells his family that he saw a dead, bloated black man pulled out of the pond. The man had been wrapped in a sheet, but a white man yanked it off, grinned, and ordered the black men to take the body into the nearby jail. While Bailey had been watching from a distance, the white man ordered him to help carry the rotting body. Once they got the body inside, the white man pretended he was going to lock in all the men but then laughed and said it was just a joke when they started to beg him not to do so. The actual prisoners were already yelling that they did not want the body in there with them, and Bailey got out as fast as he could. The young boy asks Uncle Willie and Momma why the whites hate blacks so much, but they seem to have no good answers.

In **chapter 26**, once again we see the startling contrast between the worlds of Momma and the prejudiced South and Mother and her whirlwind beauty. For six months Momma, Bailey, and Maya live in an apartment in California, waiting for their new home to be prepared for them. When Momma leaves, Maya and Bailey realize that once again they are with their beautiful stranger parent. As much as they are on edge, the children end up enraptured by Mother once again, and they realize that she too is nervous as she drives them to an apartment in Oakland where the rest of the Baxters are.

The children go to a school with amenities that their school in Stamps could never have. They are never asked by the family about their schoolwork, and instead of going to church on Sundays, they go to the movies. They find out that Mother's job is playing pinochle for money and running poker games, but she is quick to tell them she never cheats anyone. Also, they learn that only just before their arrival Mother had gotten into a fight with her business partner, with whom she had run a restaurant/casino. The fight had ended with him punching her and her shooting him twice.

Soon after the children's arrival, Mother marries Daddy Clidell, "who turned out to be the first father I would know," Angelou writes. They move with him, a successful businessman, to San Francisco.

Turmoil exists not just in the children's personal lives but in the world at large as well. World War II has started. In **chapter 27** we are told that in San Francisco the Japanese have disappeared and have been replaced with previously poor Southern blacks, who were recruited to work in the city's shipyards and ammunition plants. Ironically, these factors contribute to making Maya feel like she belongs, for she understands the collective displacement and underlying fear of always being at risk. Even though she is no longer in the South and many of the city's inhabitants believe their city to be unprejudiced, Maya says she knows otherwise. This comment and a short but biting racial story about city-dwellers make us realize Angelou is preparing us for a larger confrontation.

In **chapter 28** we are given a little more of a taste of what high school is like for Maya. Rather soon after her arrival, she transfers out of a school of brash girls to another outside of the black neighborhood, where initially she is one of only three black students. She feels a connection to the blacks as she rides the streetcars each day to and from school through the starkly differing neighborhoods. In this new school, though, Maya no longer is one of the smartest students, and most of the other students lack the fear that she has in the classroom. Although Maya is only 14, she also gets a scholarship to a college, where she takes drama and dance at night.

Another slice of the underworld is provided in **chapter 29**, in which Angelou provides a portrait of Daddy Clidell. He is uneducated but successful, owning apartment buildings and, later, pool halls. Maya admires him, and he teaches her an array of card games and introduces her to "the most successful con men in the world." The men proudly explain to her their various tricks against wealthy whites, so she will know better and never be taken by anyone herself.

This chapter serves as a superb prelude to **chapter 30**, in which Maya has to use her resources and figure the way out of a tough situation. While the previous chapter focused on a surrogate father, chapter 30 brings the young teenager back to her real father, who invites her to spend the summer with him in southern California. She is truly excited, still anticipating that he lives the good life, just as she had when he first drove into Stamps. Yet the illusion is soon destroyed when Maya arrives at her father's rather secluded trailer home, which is also inhabited by his very young girlfriend, Dolores. Maya and Dolores have a near-immediate disliking for each other, and her father seems to take pleasure in this.

Maya is surprised when her father proposes that just he and she take a trip to Mexico, where he is known to go from time to time, supposedly to pick up food for special dinners. So far Bailey Sr. has paid her little attention and not attempted to help create a pleasant vacation. Maya is excited by the trip and thinks it will be exotic and fun.

On the way to Mexico, Maya's father stops for some time to drink with a guard, and when he finally gets back in the car, he jokingly asks the guard if he wants to marry Maya. While the teenager had wanted to be introduced to her father's friends, she had never envisioned this. The guard starts grabbing her, but eventually her father takes off. They ride along twisted roads to the dirt yard of a bar, where half-naked children are chasing chickens. A group of women emerge, greeting Bailey Sr. While the women laugh when they hear that Maya is his daughter, once inside the ramshackle building everyone is quite welcoming to both of them. Maya sees her father with new eyes here. He is the center of attention and completely relaxed. Shortly she too is totally at ease, dancing and reveling with complete abandon.

The teenager then realizes she has not seen her father for some time and at first panics at the thought of having been abandoned. When she sees his car outside, she decides to wait there for him, and eventually he appears, thoroughly intoxicated, and falls fast asleep in the car. Rather than spend the night there, Maya decides she will drive them back home, assuming that she has watched enough other people drive to be able to do it herself. The teenager is exhilarated by her success and power as she finally gets the car back to the guard station. At this point she smacks into another car yet still is not afraid, just wondering whether anyone is hurt, whether her father has woken up, and what will happen next.

No one is hurt, and Maya and the passengers of the other car set about waking her snoring father. After some effort, they get him up; he assesses the situation and walks off with his insurance papers, a half-empty bottle of liquor, and the guard and the driver of the other car. In a short time, they return laughing, and Bailey Sr. gets behind the wheel as if completely recovered. Maya is quite angry that he does not praise her for her tenacity and driving and instead is oblivious to her remarkable accomplishment.

Upon their arrival back at the trailer, in **chapter 31**, Dolores almost immediately starts arguing with Bailey Sr., saying Maya has come between them. The fight escalates until Bailey leaves, slamming the door behind him. While Maya has never liked the woman, she does feel sorry for her, since her father had left Dolores behind to work and worry over what escapades the father and daughter were involved in and when they would return. Maya decides to console Dolores and feels proud of the decision, which shows what a good-hearted sort she is. Yet the end result is hardly a merciful exchange; it is a physical fight. Dolores calls Maya's mother a whore; Maya slaps her, and Dolores locks her arms around Maya, who finally shoves her away.

Once outside the trailer, Maya realizes there is blood dripping down from her waist. Dolores chases after her with a hammer, and Maya takes refuge in her father's car. Dolores is still screaming wildly when Bailey Sr. and his friends crowd around to calm her. Once Dolores is back in the trailer, the angry Bailey Sr. comes back to get into the car with Maya. She does not warn him about her blood before he sits in the puddle that has made it to the passenger's side; she gets some delight from hoping he will realize that Dolores is quite a monster.

Maya's father takes her to a friend's house to get cleaned up and bandaged, in fear that it would create too much of a scandal to go to a hospital. Afterward, he leaves Maya at another friend's house for the night, meets her in the morning with a perfunctory kiss and a dollar and a half, and says he will be back at the end of the day. Without a plan, Maya packs sandwiches and leaves.

After wandering aimlessly all day, in **chapter 32,** Maya comes to a junkyard and decides to sleep in one of the better-looking cars, feeling quite free in the open air on her own. The next day she meets the other teenage inhabitants of the junkyard, who explain the rules of their makeshift commune. Maya stays with them for a month, learning to drive, curse, and dance. But more important, Maya gains a new security by having been unconditionally accepted by peers of diverse backgrounds. Although there had been much emphasis in the beginning of the book on a need for home and a positive self-image, it takes the experience of being away from adult influence and her various homes for Maya to lose her insecurity. Her self-imposed self-reliance gives her confidence, just as it did when she drove the car with her drunken father. At least one critic has stated that Angelou's search for a home is for a place of acceptance within the self.

Maya calls her mother to get a plane ticket home (**chapter 33**). When Maya arrives in San Francisco, she realizes that it does not seem the same anymore, since she is no longer her naïve young self. We are near the end of the book, and the girl who in the prologue had so wanted to be physically transformed has indeed been transformed, but in a more profound way. She feels not so young anymore and wiser. And curiously, while her looks have not notably changed, she has become more comfortable with her physical self, after having won a dance contest with another from the junkyard and frequently going out dancing with her brother.

Maya has changed, and her brother is going through his own changes as well. He is not his usual self when she starts to tell him of her exploits in southern California, and he now has hip new friends and is even asserting his independence from their mother. Maya observes the growing confrontations between her mother and Bailey and eventually sees her 16-year-old brother take off from home in anger at one o'clock in the morning. When she talks to him the next morning in a dingy rented room a friend has found for him, Maya learns that Mother has not in fact abandoned him. Actually, he is excited to tell Maya that Mother is arranging to get him a job on the railroad. He is confident that he will succeed and work his way up. Not only has he left home, but he is taking a job that requires constant travel, perhaps feeling more at home in this instability.

Even though Maya has gained confidence during her summer exploits, she views her brother's optimism as foolhardy. She refrains from telling him so, however, and for once she appears more worldly than he. Angelou had not mentioned Bailey for a few chapters before this, preparing us for this separation. The two siblings who had been inseparable in their early years are intent on finding their own way; for Bailey, this drive is even more powerful than maintaining a close relationship with his sister.

Maya recognizes in **chapter 34** that she is so changed that she cannot go back to living her life the way she had before. Even though she is only 15, she decides to leave school and go to work, knowing her mother will admire her gumption, which Mother herself has so much of. Maya decides to get a job as a conductor on the San Francisco streetcars. Despite the fact that her mother tells her there are no blacks working on the cars, Maya decides to fight for the job, showing her again as not just her mother's daughter but as someone who must be her own self. For the most part, in Stamps there were no such opportunities for rebellion—Maya had had the pleasure of breaking her oppressive employer's dishes, but the scheme had been Bailey's and the revenge had been fleeting. Here is Maya's chance to fight and add to her now stronger self-image. She realizes she can have some control over her fate. As critics have commented, this event fits in with the slave narrative tradition, in which a confrontation with the oppressor occurs and there is a drive to achieve order out of chaos.

Maya's confrontation takes the form of daily appearances in the streetcar office, where she asks to see the personnel manager. The teenager not only forgives the clerk she constantly encounters there but sees her as a "fellow victim of the same puppeteer." Maya asks various black organizations and government officials for help in getting the job, but she gets nowhere except to allow them to slightly weaken her resilience and to get her to wonder if she truly is as mad as they believe. What allows her to finally be hired is completely unclear, but Maya does get a job as the first black conductor on the San Francisco streetcars, albeit with seemingly the least-desirable shifts. As she rides the cars proudly, she even realizes she no longer feels secure only in the black areas that they ride through.

Maya keeps the job for one semester and then goes back to school. Again she realizes that she cannot go back, that she is so much wiser and more independent than her fellow classmates. The adult Angelou's voice appears here, commenting on torturous youth. "The command to grow up at once was more bearable than the faceless horror of wavering purpose, which was youth," she writes, preparing us for what is to come in the remainder of the book.

In **chapter 35** we return to the problem of Maya's being unhappy in her body. Now she is concerned not with ugliness but with her lack of femininity, and she jumps to the conclusion that she may be a lesbian. She turns to her mother for help when she feels truly unable to discern whether she is a lesbian, even though she has read about the subject in numerous books. This shows the good comfort level that has grown between them, but when Maya ends up still questioning her sexuality not long after their conversation, we are reminded of the communication problems between the children and adults that seemed rampant in the earlier parts of the book.

We see Maya struggling further with her sexuality and growing up—some of the issues which critics have suggested gave her book universal appeal. The teenager sets her sights on finding a boyfriend, picks one of the most handsome schoolmates she knows, and offers to have sex with him. She believes this is the only way she can possibly snag a boyfriend, even temporarily.

After her sexual experience, the 16-year-old is disappointed that she has not enjoyed it and that it still does not put to rest her concerns that she may not be a normal female. Once again she turns to books, weighing her encounter against what she has read about sex and relationships in novels. In comparison, her experience was sadly lacking. The chapter ends with a one-sentence paragraph that abruptly tells us Maya is pregnant. This is a prime example of Angelou's strength as a storyteller; the surprise ending to the chapter, which is almost the last chapter in the book, compels the reader onward.

Because of the pregnancy, the teenager is consumed with fear, guilt, and self-revulsion, realizing that although for so much of her earlier life she had been like a storm-tossed ship at sea, in this instance she is nearly completely responsible for this "new catastrophe." She turns to Bailey, who has not been mentioned since the chapter in which he left home. He advises her not to tell their mother and Daddy Clidell about the pregnancy, since they will want her to leave school, and Bailey believes it would be nearly impossible for her to go back and get her diploma later. Maya takes Bailey's advice, and the evening that she graduates, she writes a note to her mother and Daddy Clidell to tell them the news. They take it in stride, although they are shocked that Maya has kept the secret for so long.

Maya has an easy delivery and admits that "possession became mixed up with motherhood." One of her overwhelming initial feelings is fear that in her awkwardness she will harm her new son. Mother recognizes this and against Maya's protests has her sleep in her bed with the baby, who is by then three weeks old. Later, when Maya is awakened by her mother, Mother tells her, "See, you don't have to think about doing the right thing. If you're for the right thing, then you do it without thinking." Mother switches the light back off, and Maya pats her baby and returns to sleep. Maya has gone through the adult experience of childbirth without having to think about it. Her mother lessens her fears, and the new mother can rest easy, putting herself in the hands of nature. Again Maya has gone through a monumental human experience while still young, and she has managed fine. We are left with peace, hopefulness, and admiration for this remarkable woman.

 Critical Views

"What are you looking at me for?
I didn't come to stay. . . ."[2]

[G]eographic movement and temporary residence become
formative aspects of [Angelou's] growing identity—equal
in importance to experiences and relationships more
commonly regarded as instrumental in forming the adult
self. Appropriately, this poetic phrase becomes the young
girl's motto or "shield" (p. 58) as Angelou calls it, Maya's
means of proclaiming her isolation while defending against its
infringement.

Shuttled between temporary homes and transient allegiances,
Maya necessarily develops a stoic flexibility that becomes not
only her "shield," but, more importantly, her characteristic
means of dealing with the world. This flexibility is both blessing
and curse: it enables her to adapt to various and changing
environments, but it also keeps her forever threatened with loss
or breakdown of her identity, as will presently be shown.

Indeed, Angelou's descriptions of her younger self seem
almost entirely composed of negatives: she is not wanted by
her parents who hold over her the unspoken, but ever-present,
threat of banishment; she is not beautiful or articulate like her
brother, Bailey; she is too introverted and passive to assert
herself on her environment; and, finally, she is a child in a
world of enigmatic adults, and a black girl in a world created by
and for the benefit of white men.

Furthermore, Maya's geographic worlds are each separate
and self-contained. There is the world of Momma and her
store in Stamps, a puritan world of racial pride, religious
devotion and acquiescence to one's worldly lot. And there is her
"wild and beautiful" mother's world of pool halls, card sharks,
fast dancing, fast talking and fast loving. Combining and

transcending both is the private and portable world of Maya's imagination.

If there is one stable element in Angelou's youth it is this dependence on books. Kipling, Poe, Austen and Thackeray, Dunbar, Johnson, Hughes and Du Bois, *The Lone Ranger*, *The Shadow* and *Captain Marvel* comics—all are equally precious to this lonely girl. Shakespeare, whose Sonnet 29 speaks to Maya's own social and emotional alienation, becomes her "first white love" (p. 11). As it does for Mary Antin, Anaïs Nin, and other female autobiographers, the public library becomes a quiet refuge from the chaos of her personal life. "I took out my first library card in St. Louis" (p. 64), she notes. And it is the public library she attempts to reach after her rape. Later, when running away from her father, she hides in a library. Indeed, when her life is in crisis, Maya characteristically escapes into the world of books.

As artifacts creating complete and meaningful universes, novels and their heroes become means by which Maya apprehends and judges her own bewildering world. Thus, Louise, her first girlfriend, reminds Maya of Jane Eyre; while Louise's mother, a domestic, Maya refers to as a governess. Mrs. Flowers, who introduces her to the magic of books, appeals to Maya because she was like "women in English novels who walked the moors . . . with their loyal dogs racing at a respectful distance. Like the women who sat in front of roaring fireplaces, drinking tea incessantly from silver trays full of scones and crumpets. Women who walked the 'heath' and read morocco-bound books and had two last names divided by a hyphen." Curiously, it is this imaginative association with a distant, extinct and colonial world that makes Mrs. Flowers one who "made me proud to be Negro, just by being herself" (p. 79).

But the plight of lovers, madmen and poets is also Maya's problem. "The little princesses who were mistaken for maids, and the long-lost children mistaken for waifs," writes Angelou, "became more real to me than our house, our mother, our school or Mr. Freeman" (p. 64). She is so consummately involved in the world of fantasy that even while being raped she "was sure any minute my mother or Bailey or the Green Hornet would burst in the door and save me" (p. 65). As in this quotation, the style by which Angelou describes her youth seems in counterpoint to the meaning of her narrative. It is written with a humor and wry wit that belies the personal and racial tragedies recorded. Since style is such a revealing element in all autobiographies, hers, especially, seems a conscious defense against the pain felt at evoking unpleasant memories. Moreover, wit operates as a formidable tool of the outraged adult; by mocking her enemies, Angelou overcomes them. Thus the gluttonous Reverend Thomas gets his just desserts at church when, "throwing out phrases like home-run balls," he loses his dentures in a scuffle with an overzealous parishioner; the self-serving condescension of "fluttering" Mrs. Cullinan is ridiculed in a "tragic ballad" on "being white, fat, old and without children"; so, too, with the vanity and carelessness of her mother's "lipstick kisses" and her father's pompous "*ers* and *errers*" as he struts among Stamps' curious "down-home folk." The adult writer's irony retaliates for the tongue-tied child's helpless pain.

The primary object, however, for Angelou's wit is herself. At times maudlin, always highly romantic and withdrawn, the young Maya is a person the older writer continually finds comic. Her idolatrous attachment to Bailey, her projections of fantasy upon reality, her reverence of her mother's stunning beauty, her strained attempts at sympathy for her self-enamoured father, her ingenuous attitude towards sexuality— these are but a few of the many and recurring aspects of her younger self the adult mocks.

The basic motive for writing one's autobiography, some believe, is to be understood, accepted, and loved. Angelou's willingness to ridicule former self-deceptions—more precisely, her former self—indicates the adult's fearlessness of the reader's judgments and her own critical stance towards herself. If Angelou's voice in re-creating her past is, therefore, ironic, it is however supremely controlled.

Nevertheless, despite the frankness of her narrative, Angelou avoids charting a direct path to her present self. Unlike *Gemini*, or *Coming of Age in Mississippi*, or *The Autobiography of Malcolm X*, or Richard Wright's *Black Boy*—books in the same genre—Angelou's autobiography barely mentions the emergent woman within the girlish actor. Although Roy Pascal believes that "the autobiographer must refer us continually outwards and onwards, to the author himself and to the outcome of all the experiences,"[3] Maya Angelou proves an exception to the rule.

Because Angelou's apprehension of experience and, indeed, herself, is essentially protean and existential, it is difficult to find one overriding identity of the adult self controlling her narrative. For what connects the adult and the child is less a linear development towards one distinct version of the self through career or philosophy, than an ever-changing multiplicity of possibilities. It is, in fact, her mutability, born of and affirmed through repeated movement, reorientation and assimilation, that becomes Angelou's unique identity, her "identity theme,"[4] to use Heinz Lichtenstein's more precise term. And if "work, in man, serves the maintenance of the individual's identity theme,"[5] as Lichtenstein asserts, then the numerous careers of the adult Angelou—as dancer, prostitute, S. C. L. C. organizer, actor, poet, journalist and director—document restlessness and resilience.

The unsettled life Angelou writes of in *I Know Why the Caged Bird Sings* suggests a sense of self as perpetually in the process of becoming, of dying and being reborn, in all its ramifications. Thus death (and to some extent its companion concept, rebirth) is the term by which her "identity theme" operates. It is the metaphor of self which most directly and comprehensively communicates Angelou's identity. . . .

When writing one's autobiography one's primary concern is the illumination of personal and historical identity while giving shape and meaning to the experiences out of which that identity has developed. Through the abyss of social and emotional death, Angelou emerges as a tenacious and vital individual.

Notes

2. Maya Angelou, *I Know Why the Caged Bird Sings* (New York: Bantam Books, 1970), 1. Subsequent page references are to this edition.

3. Roy Pascal, *Design and Truth in Autobiography* (London: Routledge & Kegan Paul Ltd., 1960), 163.

4. Heinz Lichtenstein, "Identity and Sexuality: A Study of Their Interrelationship in Man," *Journal of the American Psychoanalytic Association* 9 (1961): 208.

5. Ibid., 253.

SUSAN GILBERT ON MAYA ANGELOU: THE WRITER IN THE WRITERLY TRADITION

It is our task now to see where this book fits into several literary traditions, especially a tradition of Southern literature. For background and locale, it is hard to be more Southern than Stamps, Arkansas; St. Louis is debatable; California is OUT. Although Maya Angelou has returned to the South to become Z. Smith Reynolds Professor at Wake Forest University, it is by a very circuitous route. . . .

The South that she lived in and that her kinsmen close and distant fled makes part of her past. But she has been eager to put as much distance between herself and its white bourgeois traditions in literature as in life. The only black she speaks of with real scorn in this book is the father's priggish girlfriend who apes the ways of middle-class white women. She is a "small tight woman from the South" who "kept the house clean with the orderliness of a coffin"; who "was on close terms with her washing machine and her ironing board"; who "had all the poses of the Black bourgeoisie without the material bases to support the postures" (221). With more pity but no closer identification, she recounts that the poor black girls of Stamps were marked by the trivial traditions of Southern white women: "Ridiculous and even ludicrous. But Negro girls in small Southern towns, whether poverty-stricken or just munching along on a few of life's necessities, were given as extensive and irrelevant preparations for adulthood as rich white girls shown in magazines," the irrelevancies of "mid-Victorian values" (101). [. . .]

Although in ceasing to be Marguerite Johnson of Stamps, Arkansas, and in becoming Maya Angelou the writer, she denies the traditions—for blacks or for women—of the white South, the same themes most often called Southern fill her work. None, of course, is exclusively or originally Southern, and looking at the other traditions her work pertains to makes this very clear. . . .

As a writer she says she works from her ear, from listening to her people's cadences and habits of speech. Here she is like other Southern writers, such as Faulkner, Welty, O'Connor, Lee Smith, whose works capture the language as spoken in particular places by particular people; she differs from them in her insistence on the uniqueness of black language as the means of black survival and of triumph: "It may be enough, however, to have it said that we survive in exact relationship to the dedication of our poets (include preachers, musicians and blues singers)" (180). But she nowhere limits herself to the tongues of black Arkansas or ghetto streets. One critic has praised her "avoidance of a monolithic Black language" (O'Neale, 34) and the fact that she "does not overburden black communicants with clumsy versions of homespun black speech" (O'Neale, 35). In the white high school she attended in San Francisco, Angelou became conscious that she would use two languages: "We learned to slide out of one language and into another without being conscious of the effort. At school, in a given situation, we might respond with 'That's not unusual.' But in the street, meeting the same situation, we easily said, 'It be's like that sometimes'" (219). I have said that the point of view of the book goes back and forth between that of the inexperienced girl and the experienced writer. The language also moves between a strong, colloquial simplicity and a sometimes overblown literary mannerism. . . .

The literary traditions not often allied to Southern literature that undergird this work are those of a long Western tradition of the *bildungsroman*—a novel, often autobiographical, of a young person's growing up and finding his way among the traditions and values of the family and culture in which he or she is reared—and a long tradition in this country of Afro-American autobiography. In a sense both come together in this book; some critics have referred to it interchangeably as novel and autobiography. But the traditions are diametrically opposite in the ways the hero or heroine is portrayed.

In the *bildungsroman* the loneliness of the hero is expected. Youth is self-conscious; the hero feels that the values of his family and culture are oppressive to him; he must make his escape. It is an international genre including Goethe's *Wilhelm Meister* and James Joyce's *A Portrait of the Artist as a Young Man*, with outstanding examples in Southern literature, including Thomas Wolfe's *Look Homeward, Angel* and Richard Wright's *Native Son*. It influences women's works like Kate Chopin's *The Awakening*, and, with the publication of this first of Angelou's works in 1970 and a host of other important books that appeared in the same decade, it affects a vital new tradition in black women's writings.

Before the publication in 1940 of Wright's *Native Son*, fiction by American black writers constituted a smaller and less important body of work than the long tradition of Afro-American autobiographies arising from the narratives of escaped or redeemed slaves. In these autobiographies, the primary mode of black American prose, the role of the hero is altogether different; he is not a lonely misfit, not a rejector of his people but their exemplum. . . .

Asked this question, "Do you consider your quartet to be autobiographical novels or autobiographies?" Angelou replied, "They are autobiographies," and she went on to define her intent there as reporting on a collective, not a lone individual's story. "When I wrote *I Know Why the Caged Bird Sings*, I wasn't thinking so much about my own life or identity. I was thinking about a particular time in which I lived and the influences of that time on a number of people. I kept thinking, what about that time? What were the people around young Maya doing? I used the central figure—myself—as a focus to show how one person can make it through those times" ("Interview with Claudia Tate," 6). . . .

Two important breaks in tradition have come in the twentieth century. In 1945 Richard Wright published his autobiography, *Black Boy*, and touched off a debate that has not ended about the nature of the black experience in America.

His hero is not a random member of a group who are victims of white oppression. The white oppressors are there, but the boy suffers as much from his black family members, who have become, under the heritage of slavery, subhuman in their hunger, fear, ignorance, superstition, brutality, and despair. By the miracle of books he is awakened to a life none of his family could comprehend. Years later, as a grown man, he saw the father who laughed at his hunger, saw him as a peasant of the soil and as an animal: "how chained were his actions and emotions to the direct, animalistic impulses of his withering body" (Wright, 43). The mature Wright pitied and forgave his father, but he retained the lesson that he had to distance himself from his family or perish. Black writers especially have argued against his assertions:

> After I had outlived the shocks of childhood, after the habit of reflection had been born in me, I used to mull over the strange absence of real kindness in Negroes, how unstable was our tenderness, how lacking in genuine passion we were, how void of great hope, how timid our joy, how bare our traditions, how hollow our memories, how lacking we were in those intangible sentiments that bind man to man, and how shallow was even our despair. (Wright, 45)

Much in *I Know Why the Caged Bird Sings* and in what Angelou has said about her writing shows her in opposition to Wright's dogma. Though the girl is lonely and hurt, she finds her way to survival in terms of the traditions of her family, her mother and her grandmother, not in opposition to them. She does remark that she knew few expressions of tenderness. The grandmother was embarrassed to discuss any emotions not associated with her religious faith; the mother imparts power but not tenderness. She describes her: "Vivian Baxter had no mercy. There was a saying in Oakland at the time which, if she didn't say it herself, explained her attitude. The saying was, 'Sympathy is next to shit in the dictionary, and I can't even read.' . . . She had the impartiality of nature, with the same lack of indulgence or clemency" (201–02). In stressing her discovery of continuance of African ways among American blacks, she argues with Wright's judgment that black traditions were "bare." In her description of her use of the mode of autobiography, she says she was writing of one who typifies, not one who opposes or escapes the group.

I Know Why the Caged Bird Sings appeared in 1970. In the same year appeared Toni Morrison's *The Bluest Eye*, Alice Walker's *The Third Life of Grange Copeland*, Louise Meriwether's *Daddy Was a Numbers Runner*, Michele Wallace's *Black Macho and the Myth of the Superwoman*, and Nikki Giovanni's *Black Feeling, Black Talk/Black Judgement.* In these and other notable works of the 1970s—including Ntozake Shange's *For Colored Girls Who Have Considered Suicide/When the Rainbow Is Enuf* (Broadway, 1976)—black women writers have debated the effects of black sexism, and many have asserted that they must find their identity not merely in opposition to the traditions for the woman that the black culture imposes.

Angelou has put herself apart consistently from the movement of white women's liberation. Black women, she says, have never been as subservient within their community as white women in theirs: "White men, who are in effect their fathers, husbands, brothers, their sons, nephews and uncles, say to white women, or imply in any case: 'I don't really need you to run my institutions. I need you in certain places and in those places you must be kept—in the bedroom, in the kitchen, in the nursery, and on the pedestal.' Black women have never been told this" ("Interview with Claudia Tate," 3). Though they have not occupied the pulpits, black women have been leaders in their communities, according to Angelou. She is pleased with the dialogue that these black women's works have begun. . . .

I Know Why the Caged Bird Sings is sixteen years old now, the experience it recounts more than forty years old. Yet nothing, it seems, could be more timely.

It is an admirable story; and it is not typical. Typically the black girl who has no permanent father in her home; who is shuffled between mother and grandmother, city and country; who is raped at eight, a mother at sixteen; who supports her child, without help from its father or from her own mother, with odd jobs, waitressing, bartending, prostitution—typically such girls do not become *Ladies Home Journal's* Woman of the Year for Communications or Z. Smith Reynolds Professor at Wake Forest University or recipients of a dozen honorary degrees. For all Angelou's heroic assertion that the black woman emerges victorious from oppression and abuse, most of them do not. They are not equipped to succeed by any of the traditions here laid out—not that of the dominant white bourgeoisie, which taught a generation of Southern women, black and white, to sew and crochet and be debutantes; not that of the pious black churchwomen who look for reward and vindication in the next life; not that of the black streets where one of her mother's boyfriends was kicked to death and another one shot and where Angelou once herself took a pistol to the home of a boy who had threatened her son. Few black women have had work so well for them the swift vengeance outside the law; they have been victims of lawlessness as cruel as the law that first held them oppressed and then neglected their victimization.

Angelou knows it is a heroic, not a typical, model. The dedication, you remember, is to her son and to "all the strong Black birds of promise who defy the odds and gods."

One last note. Bearing the emphasis on family with tradition we have seen common to Southern literature, this book bears no mark of the provincialism of which not only Southern literature but much of American literature of recent decades, especially the literature of American women, has been accused.

Non-American writers such as Salman Rushdie and Nadine Gordimer complained loudly that ours has become a literature of the misunderstood individual. It abounds in complaints and self-centered preoccupations (will the heroine, like Gail Godwin's Odd Woman, achieve orgasm); it finds little room for the hunger of the children of the world or for the brutalities of police states.

Artistically Maya Angelou may err on the side of didacticism, but she is free of exaggerated self-concern. The voice in the story shifts from the girl of limited experience and perspective to that of the writer who speaks with the authority of truths gleaned from traditions as diverse as Shakespeare and Ghanian folk tale. By her work she has not only contributed to but also expanded the American literary tradition and the perspective from which this literature views—and serves—the world.

CAROL E. NEUBAUER INTERVIEWS ANGELOU ABOUT WRITING AUTOBIOGRAPHY

ANGELOU: Autobiography is for me a beloved which, like all beloveds, one is not given by family. One happens upon. You know, you turn the corner to the left instead of to the right. Stop in the parking lot and meet a beloved, or someone who becomes a beloved. And by the time I was half finished with *Caged Bird* I knew I loved the form—that I wanted to try to see what I could do with the form. Strangely enough, not as a cathartic force, not really; at any rate I never thought that really I was interested or am interested in autobiography for its recuperative power. I liked the form—the literary form—and by the time I started *Gather Together* I had gone back and reread Frederick Douglass' slave narrative. Anyway, I love the idea of the slave narrative, using the first person singular, really meaning always the third person plural. I love that. And I see it all the time in the black literature, in the blues and spirituals and the poetry, in essays James Baldwin uses it. But I've tried in each book to let the new voice come through and that's what makes it very difficult for me not to impose the voice of 1980 onto the voice I'm writing from 1950, possibly.

NEUBAUER: And so when you say you look for a new voice you don't mean the voice of the present or the time of writing the autobiographical account, but rather of that period of your past. That must be difficult.

ANGELOU: Very. Very difficult, but I think that in writing autobiography that that's what is necessary to really move it from almost an "as told to" to an "as remembered" state. And really for it to be a creative and artistic literary art form. . . .

NEUBAUER: One of the things I'm interested in particularly is how the present influences the autobiographical past. I think what you're engaged in doing now and have been since *Caged Bird* is something that's never been done before in this scope. Each volume of yours is a whole and has a unity that works for that volume alone. If you were to go back to the period of *Caged Bird* that would add another wrinkle in this question of time and different voices.

ANGELOU: I don't know how I will do it, and I don't know if I'll be able to do it. But I think there are facets. When I look at a stained glass window, it's very much like this book. I have an idea that the books are very much like the Everyman stories so that there is greed and kindness and generosity and cruelty, oppression, and sloth. And I think of the period I'm going to write about and I try to see which of the incidents in which greed, say it's green, which of these that happened to me during that period will most demonstrate that particular condition. Now some are more rich, but I refuse them. I do not select them because it's very hard to write drama without falling into melodrama. So the incidents I reject, I find myself unable to write about without becoming melodramatic. I just can't see how to write it. In *Gather Together* there is an incident in which a man almost killed me—tried to, in fact—and kept me for three days and he was a mad man, literally. My escape was so incredible, literally incredible, that there was no way to write it, absolutely, to make it credible and not melodramatic.

NEUBAUER: Have you ever chosen to take another incident in that case, perhaps one that might not have even happened, and use that as a substitute?

ANGELOU: No, because there were others which worked, which did happen, and which showed either cruelty or the irony of escape. So I was able to write that rather than the other.

NEUBAUER: I see. So you didn't have to sacrifice the core of the experience.

ANGELOU: No, I never sacrificed. It's just choosing which of those greens or which of those reds to make that kind of feeling.

NEUBAUER: It's a beautiful metaphor, the greens, the reds and the light coming through the window. Because in a sense, memory works that way; it filters out past work. And yet an autobiographer has a double task—at least double, probably triple or quadruple—in some ways the filtering has been done beyond your control on an unconscious level. But as a writer working in the present you, too, are making selections or choices, which complicate the experience.

ANGELOU: There is so much to talk to you about on this subject. I have, I think, due to all those years of not talking, which again, I chose to minimize in *Caged Bird* because it's hard to write that without, again, the melodramas leaking in. But because of those years of muteness, I think my memory was developed in queer ways, because I remember—I have total recall—or I have none at all. None. And there is no pattern to the memory, so that I would forget all the good and the bad of a certain time, or I will remember *only* the bad of a certain time, or I will remember *only* the good. But when I remember it, I will remember *everything* about it. *Everything*. The outside noises, the odors in the room, the way my clothes were feeling—everything. I just have it, or I remember nothing. I am sure that is a part of the sort of psychological problems I was having and how the memory went about its business knitting itself.

NEUBAUER: Almost as a treasure chest or a defense.

ANGELOU: Yes, both, I guess. But in a sense, not really a defense, because some of the marvelous things I've not remembered. For instance, one of the promises I've exacted from every lover or husband who promised to be a permanent fixture was that *if* I die in the house, if something happened, get me outside. Please don't let me die in the room, or open the window and let me see some rolling hills. Let me see, please. Now, my memory of Stamps, Arkansas, is flat, dirt, the trees around the pond. But everything just flat and mean. When I agreed to go to join Bill Moyers for his creativity program, I flew to Dallas and decided to drive to Stamps because I wanted to sneak up on Stamps. It's, I guess, 200 miles or more. When I drove out of Texas into Arkansas, Stamps is 30 miles from Texas. I began to see the undulating hills. I couldn't believe it! I couldn't believe it! It's beautiful! It's what I love. But the memory had completely gone.

NEUBAUER: When you're working . . . are there things that help you remember . . . the past better? . . . Is it a frightening journey because of the deep roots from that time to the present? Do you feel a kind of vulnerability? . . .

ANGELOU: I am not afraid of the ties. I cherish them, rather. It's the vulnerability. It's like using drugs or something. It's allowing oneself to be hypnotized. That's frightening, because then we have no defenses, nothing. We've slipped down the well and every side is slippery. And how on earth are you going to come out? That's scary. But I've chosen it, and I've chosen this mode as my mode.

ELIZABETH FOX-GENOVESE ON
BREAKING OUT OF THE CAGE OF RACISM

I Know Why the Caged Bird Sings. The fracturing of slavery's shackles formally freed individuals, but left blacks as a people caged. Unbreakable bars closed black communities in upon themselves, denying both the communities and the individuals who composed them access to the surrounding white world. Within those cages, black communities developed their own vibrant life, black women raised up black girls in the way that they should go. Singing in the face of danger, singing to thwart the stings of insolence, singing to celebrate their Lord, singing to testify to a better future, singing with the life blood of their people, black women defied their imprisonment. The cages constrained, but did not stifle them. The songs of confinement grounded the vitality of their tradition, launched the occasional fledgling to freedom. . . .

Slavery days are long gone, but their traces linger, shooting up like those uncontrollable weeds that can eat up a garden in the course of a summer. Even during slavery, free black communities flourished in the North and in pockets of the South. But the very name "free black" belies those communities' freedom from the heavy hand of slavery as a social system and indexes their ties to the South. The tradition of African-American autobiography began, in William L. Andrews's phrase, as the determination "to tell a free story."[2] The obsession with freedom betokened the indissoluble, if submerged, obsession with slavery. Race grounded the association. In a country in which only black people were enslaved, blackness and unfreedom merged in a shadowy negation of the virtues of freedom. Slavery grounded and guaranteed racism. Slavery confirmed the association between freedom and virtue, between freedom and whiteness, between whiteness and virtue. Slavery negated the individualism of blacks singly, negated the autonomy of blacks as a community. And these very negations ineluctably bound "free" blacks to the history of their enslaved brothers and sisters. In dissociating themselves from the condition of their enslaved people, they risked dissociating themselves from their people—from their race.

In the roads and cages of the South, during slavery times as thereafter, lay the history—the pre-history—of each and every black self. These roads and cages embodied the specific history that made the black self a singular self, rather than an accidental exemplar of some archetypical self. Only through recuperation of that history could African-American men and women represent their discrete selves as whole and free. The challenge of representing a metaphysically free yet historically specific self proved daunting, although never insurmountable.[3] And if daunting for black men, how much more so for black women? For if black men confronted the specific challenge of demonstrating their manhood in a culture that viewed enslavement as the negation not only of freedom but of manly virtue, black women remained torn between demonstrating their virtuous womanhood and their individualism. The pressures to opt for the demonstration of true womanhood were strong. Many black men accepted the values of white society that held that a dependent and subservient woman offered stellar proof of a man's manhood. Many white women expected black women faithfully to adhere to white culture's images of true womanhood as retiring and self-abnegating. But professed dependence and self-denial threw black women back into the arms of slavery, even if now in the service of their own people.

Gender, race, and condition wove a tight web around black women's possibilities for self-representation, especially since for them, as for their men, any understanding of the self led back over dusty roads to Southern cages.[4] Worse, the conventions of womanhood that whites had developed and middle-class blacks apparently embraced branded the very act of authorship as pushy and unfeminine. As women and as blacks, African-American women autobiographers were, in some measure, bound to construct their self-representations through available discourses, and in interaction with intended readers. For them, as for white women and for white and black men, the self had to be represented in the (recognizable) discourses of one or more interpretive communities. To be sure, their self-representations could variously—and even simultaneously—comply with, subvert, or transform prevailing discourses. But the abiding danger persisted of seeing themselves through the prism of a (white) androcentric discourse, literally through men's eyes, through white eyes.

At the beginning of the twentieth century, American culture knew no black discourse of Southern roads and cages. The discourses existed, but did not figure prominently—and certainly not independently—in the dominant discourses of the country. Here and there a bit of dialect would surface, here and there a trace of song, but almost always through the objectifying consciousness of a white observer. The music, the tales, the speech of black communities remained largely confined to the Southern oral culture in which it flowered.[5] In *Caged Bird*, Maya Angelou recalls the double language of her teens:

> My education and that of my Black associates were quite different from the education of our white schoolmates. In the classroom we all learned past participles, but in the streets and in our homes the Blacks learned to drop s's from plurals and suffixes from past-tense verbs. We were alert to the gap separating the written word from the colloquial. We learned to slide out of one language and into another without being conscious of the effort. At school, in a given situation, we might respond with "That's not unusual." But in the street, meeting the same situation, we easily said, "It be's like that sometimes." (219)

It required education in the dominant (white) speech for her to recognize the black language of the streets, and beyond it the language of Stamps, as distinct. Without immersion in white culture, she would never have recognized the distinctiveness of the speech of her people, would simply have accepted it as a given. Similarly, Hurston remembered the chinaberry blossoms of Eatonville and that, as a child, she had "loved the fleshy, white fragrant blooms" but had not made too much of them. "They were too common in my neighborhood." But when she got to New York she "found out that the people called them gardenias, and that the flowers cost a dollar each" and was impressed (18). Black American speech has penetrated the dominant culture through the writings of literate blacks who have recuperated the oral culture of their people through the prism of that dominant culture, which has suggested new ways of seeing, writing, interpreting that culture. And, for African-American autobiographers in particular, the culture of their people has remained the seedbed of their origins as selves. But when they have written of that culture, they inescapably have written as exiles. Their very writing betokens the chasm that separates them from folk culture as oral culture.

In different ways, Zora Neale Hurston and Maya Angelou broke ground for new representations of the African-American female self. *Dust Tracks*, published in 1942, and *Caged Bird*, published in 1969, explicitly reclaim the Southern past as the grounding of their authors' identities. Both explicitly reject white norms of womanhood as models. In Hurston's pages, the Southern past reemerges as a mythic past suitable for the unique self; in Angelou's pages, it acquires a historical and sociological specificity that helps to account for the modern strength of the female self as survivor. . . .

"I hadn't so much forgot as I couldn't bring myself to remember" (3). *I Know Why the Caged Bird Sings* begins with memory and its lapses. Maya Angelou represents her young self as unable to remember the remainder of a poem. The poem that the younger self could not remember began, "What are you looking at me for? / I didn't come to stay . . ." (3). The line she could not remember went, "I just come to tell you, it's Easter Day" (5). Angelou thus opens *Caged Bird* under the aegis of memory, truth, and passing through. The "n[o]t stay[ing]" of the poem recited by the children in the Colored Methodist Episcopal Church in Stamps, Arkansas, referred to the reality of resurrection from the brevity and immateriality of life on this troubled earth to a better life. Yet in Angelou's hands, the poem also evokes a secular meaning. Surely, her younger self had not come to Stamps to stay. Was she not merely passing time before rejoining her parents, claiming her birthright, embarking on a better life?

For the young Marguerite, the birthright she would one day claim is her own whiteness. Watching her grandmother make her dress for that Easter day, she had known "that once I put it on I'd look like a movie star," would "look like one of the sweet little white girls who were everybody's dream of what was right with the world." But the light of Easter morning harshly reveals the magic dress to be only "a plain ugly cut-down from a white woman's once-was-purple throwaway." Yet Marguerite clings to the truth of her own resurrection: "Wouldn't they be surprised when one day I woke out of my black ugly dream . . . ?" (4). It was all a dreadful mistake. "Because I was really white and because a cruel fairy stepmother, who was understandably jealous of my beauty, had turned me into a too-big Negro girl, with nappy black hair, broad feet and a space between her teeth that would hold a number two pencil" (4–5). And Angelou, the narrator, notes, bringing her adult knowledge to bear on the memories, "If growing up is painful for the Southern Black girl, being aware of her displacement is the rust on the razor that threatens the throat. It is an unnecessary insult" (6).

In *Caged Bird*, Angelou sifts through the pain to reappropriate—on her own terms—that Southern past and to undo the displacement. Her highly crafted, incandescent text selectively explores the intertwining relations of origins and memory to her identity. The unrecognized whiteness of the child she represents herself as having been gives way to the proud blackness of the woman she has become. The pride is the pride of a survivor, of history repossessed. That "the adult American Negro female emerges a formidable character," she insists, should be "accepted as an inevitable outcome of the struggle won by survivors" (265).

In her brief opening prologue, Angelou establishes both her perspective as adult narrator—the survivor of the memories of which she is writing—and the perspective of the child she recollects herself as having been. As a child she presumably experienced the world around her in a seamless flow, punctuated by disconnected fragments, like a young girl's traumatic inability to control her urine. The adult narrator captures the emblematic memories, vivid and compelling in themselves, and weaves them together to illustrate and anchor the truth of the story as a whole. The prologue thus offers a concrete identification of the protagonist as black, Southern female—the interpreter of her own experience, the teller of her own story.

Notes

2. Andrews, in *To Tell a Free Story*, emphasizes nineteenth-century African-Americans' concern with freedom in their self-representations, but the relation between freedom and the independent self figures in most discussions of the slave narrative. See, for example, Sekora and Turner; Davis and Gates; Foster; Smith, *Where I'm Bound*; Baker; and Stepto. The theme of freedom and selfhood was unquestionably important to Frederick Douglass and Harriet Jacobs. See Martin; Yellin's introduction to Jacobs's *Incidents*; and my epilogue to *Within the Plantation Household*.

3. Barbara McCaskill offers a pioneering exploration of the relations between African-American women's self-representations and the expectations of their readerships. Henry Louis Gates's welcome 30-volume *Schomburg Library* offers a newly coherent picture of African-American women's writings, and the authors of the introductions to the discrete volumes offer important discussions of the specific texts.

4. I have offered a fuller discussion of the nature of African-American women's experience and self-representations in relation to gender, especially their sense of gender identity, in "To Write My Self" and *Within the Plantation Household*.

5. For a thorough and thoughtful discussion of black folk culture, see Levine. For examples of white evocation of black dialect, see Harriet Beecher Stowe's *Uncle Tom's Cabin* (1852). Significantly, Jacobs, in *Incidents*, represents slave women on the plantation as speaking in dialect, but herself as speaking perfect "white" English.

ONITA ESTES-HICKS ON ANGELOU'S REDEMPTIVE VIEW OF THE SOUTH

Following its publication in 1945, Richard Wright's immortal *Black Boy* served for decades as a paradigm for Black South autobiography. Closely allied to the slave narrative in content and in structure, Wright's masterpiece, like Douglass's classic narrative of his bondage and freedom, focuses on the "fortunate fall" of his younger self, whose precociousness and innate sense of dignity rendered him unfit for the unfreedom of the segregated South. . . .

Like the classic slave narrative, *Black Boy* concludes with its brutalized hero bound for safer ground in the North, its immemorial lyricism anticipating relief from the harsh conditions of oppression in the Black South:

> I was leaving the South to fling myself into the unknown, to meet other situations that would perhaps elicit from me other responses. And if I could meet enough of a different life, then, perhaps, gradually and slowly I might learn who I was, what I might be. (228)

As their titles sometimes reflect, post–*Black Boy* autobiographical writings by refugees from the Black South continued to bemoan the homeland as wasteland and as enemy territory. Fashioned in the bondage-freedom structure which Sidonie Smith has discerned at work in the African American autobiographical tradition, these texts also stressed the necessity of flight from the feared fatherland—featuring their authors as homeless in the native land. . . .

Marked by a pattern of bondage-flight-freedom, these deeply moving autobiographical reflections by native sons and native daughters of the South conceded the irrevocable loss of the land of nativity, accepting flight and natal alienation as the necessary terms for survival and success in surrogate homelands.

A product of the third period of African American autobiography (Butterfield), and building upon first- and second-period paradigms classically represented by Douglass and Wright respectively, Maya Angelou's *I Know Why the Caged Bird Sings* (1970) inaugurated a new phase of reminiscences about experiences in the Black South. Faithfully and fatefully portraying the horrors of the old, apartheid South, the dominant theme of earlier black autobiography, Angelou's record of her formative years in Stamps, Arkansas, backgrounded a positive vision of an autonomous black community centered in the economic independence of Mrs. Annie Henderson, the author's resilient paternal grandmother. Parallelled in other "third-period" autobiographical writings of the seventies, Angelou's autobiographical mode, while foregrounding the South as what Baraka has characterized as "the scene of the crime" (95), imparts an emerging yet tentative measure of acceptance of the once reviled region. . . .

Maya Angelou, in her popular *I Know Why the Caged Bird Sings*, attributes her youthful departure from the South, which served as home to her and her beloved brother Bailey, to their wise grandmother's concern for Bailey's safety after a local white forced Angelou's fourteen-year-old sibling to assist in disposing of the body of a "dead and rotten" black male (192). While documenting the "forced-flight" pattern of earlier Black South autobiographies and acknowledging the "burden of impotent pain" which Jean Toomer so movingly captured in his autobiographical *Cane*, Angelou was to pay homage to that soulful beauty which Toomer himself had found in the old apartheid South during his brief 1922 sojourn in Sparta, Georgia. Joanne Braxton's study *Black Women Writing Autobiography* calls attention to *Caged Bird*'s radiant remembrances of things past in Stamps, Arkansas, tracing Angelou's vision of nurturing family and cohesive community to postgyneric influences in the genre of autobiography.

Punctuated by life-sustaining community rituals involving church gatherings, storytelling sessions in the family-owned store, and cooperative work projects (such as annual hog slaughterings, preserving and canning activities, and work in the cotton fields), Angelou's poignant portraits of her immediate family's orderly daily life suggest some measure of the stability which graced the lives of Black Southerners based on the mutual need, reciprocal respect, and shared compassion which oppression encouraged. Maya's grandmother's store, "the lay center of activities in town" (7), gave the writer a Hurston-like post from which to observe the rich life of small-town Arkansas in the thirties during her ten-year stay in the South:

> In those tender mornings the Store was full of laughing, joking, boasting and bragging. One man was going to pick two hundred pounds of cotton, and another three hundred. Even the children were promising to bring home fo' bits and six bits. (9)

OPAL MOORE ON THE COURAGE
TO READ *CAGED BIRD*

I Know Why the Caged Bird Sings, the autobiography of Maya Angelou, is the story of one girl's growing up. But, like any literary masterpiece, the story of this one black girl declaring "I can" to a color-coded society that in innumerable ways had told her "you can't, you won't" transcends its author. It is an affirmation; it promises that life, if we have the courage to live it, will be worth the struggle. A book of this description might seem good reading for junior high and high school students. According to People for the American Way, however, *Caged Bird* was the ninth "most frequently challenged book" in American schools (Graham 26).[1] *Caged Bird* elicits criticism for its honest depiction of rape, its exploration of the ugly spectre of racism in America, its recounting of the circumstances of Angelou's own out-of-wedlock teen pregnancy, and its humorous poking at the foibles of the institutional church. Arguments advocating that *Caged Bird* be banned from school reading lists reveal that the complainants, often parents, tend to regard any treatment of these kinds of subject matter in school as inappropriate—despite the fact that the realities and issues of sexuality and violence, in particular, are commonplace in contemporary teenage intercourse and discourse. The children, they imply, are too innocent for such depictions; they might be harmed by the truth.

This is a curious notion—that seriousness should be banned from the classroom while beyond the classroom, the irresponsible and sensational exploitation of sexual, violent, and profane materials is as routine as the daily dose of soap opera. . . .

[W]hat young readers seem most innocent of these days is not sex, murder, or profanity, but concepts of self-empowerment, faith, struggle as quest, the nobility of intellectual inquiry, survival, and the nature and complexity of moral choice. *Caged Bird* offers these seemingly abstract (adult) concepts to a younger audience that needs to know that their lives are not inherited or predestined, that they can be participants in an exuberant struggle to subjugate traditions of ignorance and fear. Critics of this book might tend to overlook or devalue the necessity of such insights for the young. *Caged Bird*'s critics imply an immorality in the work based on the book's images. However, it is through Angelou's vivid depictions of human spiritual triumph *set against a backdrop* of human weakness and failing that the autobiography speaks dramatically about moral choice. Angelou paints a picture of some of the negative choices: white America choosing to oppress groups of people; choosing lynch law over justice; choosing intimidation over honor. She offers, however, "deep talk" on the possibility of positive choices: choosing life over death (despite the difficulty of that life); choosing courage over safety; choosing discipline over chaos; choosing voice over silence; choosing compassion over pity, over hatred, over habit; choosing work and planning and hope over useless recrimination and slovenly despair. The book's detractors seem unwilling to admit that morality is not edict (or an innate property of innocence), but the learned capacity for judgment, and that the necessity of moral choice arises only in the presence of the soul's imperfection.

Self-empowerment, faith, struggle as quest, survival, intellectual curiosity, complexity of choice—these ideas are the underpinning of Maya Angelou's story. To explore these themes, the autobiography poses its own set of oppositions: traditional society and values vs. contemporary society and its values; silence vs. self expression; literacy vs. the forces of oppression; the nature of generosity vs. the nature of cruelty; spirituality vs. ritual. Every episode of *Caged Bird*, engages these and other ideas in Maya Angelou's portrait of a young girl's struggle against adversity—a struggle against rape: rape of the body, the soul, the mind, the future, of expectation, of tenderness—toward identity and self-affirmation. If we cannot delete rape from our lives, should we delete it from a book about life?

Caged Bird opens with the poignant, halting voice of Marguerite Johnson, the young Maya Angelou, struggling for her own voice beneath the vapid doggerel of the yearly Easter pageant:

"What you lookin at me for?"
"I didn't come to stay. . . ."

These two lines prefigure the entire work. "What you lookin at me for . . ." is the painful question of every black girl made self-conscious and self-doubting by a white world critical of her very existence. The claim that she "didn't come to stay" increases in irony as the entire work ultimately affirms the determination of Marguerite Johnson and, symbolically, all of the unsung survivors of the Middle Passage, to do that very thing—to stay. To stay is to affirm life and the possibility of redemption. To stay—despite the circumstance of our coming (slavery), despite the efforts to remove us (lynching) or make us invisible (segregation). . . .

When asked why she included the rape in her autobiography, Angelou has said, "I wanted people to see that the man was not totally an ogre (*Conversations*, 156). And it is this fact that poses one of the difficulties of rape and the inability of children, intellectually unprepared, to protect themselves. If the rapists were all terrible ogres and strangers in dark alleys, it would be easier to know when to run, when to scream, when to "say no." But the devastation of rape is subtle in its horror and betrayal that creates in Marguerite feelings of complicity in her own assault. When queried by Mr. Freeman's defense attorney about whether Mr. Freeman had ever touched her on occasions before the rape, Marguerite, recalling that first encounter, realizes immediately something about the nature of language, its inflexibility, its inability to render the whole truth, and the palpable danger of being misunderstood:

I couldn't . . . tell them how he had loved me once for a few minutes and how he had held me close before he thought I had peed in my bed. My uncles would kill me and Grandmother Baxter would stop speaking, as she often did when she was angry. And all those people in the court would stone me as they had stoned the harlot in the Bible. And Mother, who thought I was such a good girl, would be so disappointed. But most important, there was Bailey. I had kept a big secret from him. (70–71)

To protect herself, Marguerite lies: "Everyone in the court knew that the answer had to be No. Everyone except Mr. Freeman and me" (71).

Some schools that have chosen not to ban *Caged Bird* completely have compromised by deleting "those rape chapters." It should be clear, however, that this portrayal of rape is hardly titillating or "pornographic." It raises issues of trust, truth and lie, love, the naturalness of a child's craving for human contact, language and understanding, and the confusion engendered by the power disparities that necessarily exist between children and adults. . . .

Caged Bird, in this scene so often deleted from classroom study, opens the door for discussion about the prevalent confusion between a young person's desire for affection and sexual invitation. Certainly, this is a valuable distinction to make and one that young men and women are often unable to perceive or articulate. Angelou also reveals the manner by which an adult manipulates a child's desire for love as a thin camouflage for his own crude motives. A further complication to the neat assignment of blame is that Marguerite's lie is not prompted by a desire to harm Mr. Freeman but by her feelings of helplessness and dread. Yet, she perceives that the effect of that lie is profound—so profound that she decides to stop her own voice, both as penance for the death of Mr. Freeman and out of fear of the power of her words: " . . . a man was dead because I had lied" (72).

This dramatization of the ambiguity of truth and the fearfulness of an Old Testament justice raises questions of justice and the desirability of truth in a world strapped in fear, misunderstanding, and the inadequacy of language. The story reveals how violence can emerge out of the innocent routines of life; how betrayal can be camouflaged with blame; that adults are individual and multi-dimensional and flawed; but readers also see how Marguerite overcomes this difficult and alienating episode of her life.

Note

1. Joyce Graham, in her dissertation "The Freeing of Maya Angelou's *Caged Bird*," offers a comprehensive overview of the history of censorship efforts directed specifically against *Caged Bird*: the issues and arguments raised in connection with the teaching of the work, a look at the National Council of Teachers of English's efforts to provide guidelines for the improvement of teacher preparation in the teaching of literature, and a case study of one well documented censorship challenge. Dr. Graham also includes an interview with Dr. Angelou discussing the nature and motive of censorship. This timely examination of the rising fear of literature in schools provides an invaluable look at the parents and administrators behind the news reports on censorship challenges.

PIERRE A. WALKER ON ARTISTIC STYLE AND POLITICAL MESSAGE IN *CAGED BIRD*

Angelou does not elaborate on how she distinguishes literary autobiography from any other kind of autobiography, and of course, for a poststructuralist, the challenge to write *literary* rather than "ordinary" autobiography is meaningless because there is no difference between the two (see Eagleton, 201). For a formalist aesthetic, however, the distinctive qualities and characteristics of literary or poetic language as opposed to ordinary language are central operative concerns (see Brooks, 729–31; Shklovsky, 12; Fish, 68–96). Cleanth Brooks's belief that "the parts of a poem are related to each other organically, and related to the total theme indirectly" (730) was a primary tenet of interpretation for American New Critics, ultimately related to their determination to distinguish literary from ordinary language. Poststructuralism in its most vehemently antiformalist manifestations usually belittles Brooks's beliefs in organic unity and in the uniqueness of literary language, but criticisms of formalism and of "literature" as a distinct and privileged category, so typical of much poststructuralist theorizing, become specially problematic in relation to African-American literature.

Many African-American texts were written to create a particular political impact. As a result, one can hardly ignore either the political conditions in which the slave narratives and Richard Wright's early works, for example, were composed or the political impact their authors (and editors and publishers, at least of the slave narratives) intended them to have. Even African-American texts that are not obviously part of a protest tradition are received in a political context, as is clear from the tendency in much critical commentary on Zora Neale Hurston to demonstrate an elusive element of protest in her novels.

So important is the political to the experience of African-American literature that it comes as no surprise that the increasing incorporation of the African-American literary tradition into mainstream academic literary studies since 1980 coincides exactly with the increasingly greater significance of the political in the prevailing critical paradigm. . . .

The problem is that African-American literature has, on more than one occasion, relied on confirming its status as literature to accomplish its political aims. Since slavery relied on a belief that those enslaved were not really human beings, slave narrators responded by writing books that emphasized the fact that they themselves were humans who deserved to be treated as such. Since emancipation, African-American authors have used the same strategy to fight the belief in racial hierarchies that relegated them to second-class citizen status. One way to do this was to produce "high art," which was supposed to be one of the achievements of the highest orders of human civilization. African-American poetry provides many examples of this strategy: Claude McKay's and Countee Cullen's reliance on traditional, European poetic forms and James Weldon Johnson's "O Black and Unknown Bards." Cullen's "Yet Do I Marvel," for instance, relies on recognizable English "literary" features: Shakespearean sonnet form, rhyme, meter, references to Greek mythology, and the posing of a theological question as old as the Book of Job and as familiar as William Blake's "The Tyger."

Thus for a critical style to dismiss the closely related categories of form and of literature is to relegate to obscurity an important tradition of African-American literature and an important political tool of the struggle in the United States of Americans of African descent. This is clearly true in respect to *Caged Bird*, which displays the kind of literary unity that would please Brooks, but to the significant political end of demonstrating how to fight racism. Angelou wrote *Caged Bird* in the late 1960s at the height of the New Criticism, and therefore in order for it to be the *literary* autobiography . . . Angelou's book had to display features considered at the time typical of literature, such as organic unity. This is a political gesture, since in creating a text that satisfies contemporary criteria of "high art," Angelou underscores one of the book's central themes: how undeservedly its protagonist was relegated to second-class citizenship in her early years. To ignore form in discussing Angelou's book, therefore, would mean ignoring a critical dimension of its important political work.

Because scholarly discussions of Angelou's autobiographical works have only appeared in any significant number in the last fifteen years, *Caged Bird* and her other books have avoided—or, depending on one's view, been spared—the kind of formal analysis typically associated with New Criticism or Structuralism.[2] Scholarly critics of *Caged Bird*, often influenced by feminist and African-American studies, have focused on such issues as whether the story of Angelou's young protagonist is personal or universal, or on race, gender, identity, displacement, or a combination of these. In relation to these issues, they discuss important episodes like the scene with the "powhitetrash" girls, young Maya's rape and subsequent muteness, her experience with Mrs. Flowers, the graduation, the visit to the dentist, Maya's month living in a junkyard, or her struggle to become a San Francisco streetcar conductor.[3] What they do not do is analyze these episodes as Angelou constructed them—often juxtaposing disparate incidents within an episode—and arranged and organized them, often undermining the chronology of her childhood . . . and juxtaposing the events of one chapter with the events of preceding and following ones so that they too comment on each other. The critics do not explore how Angelou, who has never denied the principle of selection in the writing of autobiography,[4] shaped the material of her childhood and adolescent life story in *Caged Bird* to present Maya's first sixteen years, much as a *bildungsroman* would, as a progressive process of affirming identity, learning about words, and resisting racism.[5] What scholars have focused on in *Caged Bird* does merit attention, but an attention to the formal strategies Angelou uses to emphasize what the book expresses about identity and race reveals a sequence of lessons about resisting racist oppression, a sequence that leads Maya progressively from helpless rage and indignation to forms of subtle resistance and finally to outright and active protest.

The progression from rage and indignation to subtle resistance to active protest gives *Caged Bird* a thematic unity that stands in contrast to the otherwise episodic quality of the narrative. To claim thematic unity is to argue that form and content work together, an assertion that is anathema to much current literary theory. However, the formal in *Caged Bird* is the vehicle of the political, and not analyzing this text formally can limit one's appreciation of how it intervenes in the political. Critics should not focus on the political at the expense of the formal but instead should see the political and the formal as inextricably related. . . .

Caged Bird's commentators have discussed how episodic the book is, but these episodes are crafted much like short stories, and their arrangement throughout the book does not always follow strict chronology.[7] Nothing requires an autobiography to be chronological, but an expectation of chronology on the reader's part is normal in a text that begins, as *Caged Bird* does, with earliest memories. Nevertheless, one of the most important early episodes in *Caged Bird* comes much earlier in the book than it actually did in Angelou's life: the scene in which the "powhitetrash" girls taunt Maya's grandmother takes up the book's fifth chapter, but it occurred when Maya "was around ten years old" (23), two years after Mr. Freeman rapes her (which occurs in the twelfth chapter).

Situating the episode early in the book makes sense in the context of the previous chapters: the third chapter ends with Angelou describing her anger at the "used-to-be-sheriff" who warned her family of an impending Klan ride (14–15), and the fourth chapter ends with her meditation on her early inability to perceive white people as human (20–21). The scene with the "powhitetrash" girls follows this (24–27), indicating how nonhuman white people can be. But if that was all that motivated the organization of her episodes, Angelou could as easily have followed the meditation on white people's nonhumanity with the episode in which young Maya breaks the china of her white employer, Mrs. Cullinan. What really organizes chapters three through five is Angelou's presentation of the futility of indignation and the utility of subtle resistance as ways of responding to racism.

Notes

2. A search in the MLA computerized databank reveals forty-four items on Angelou, with the oldest dating back to 1973, three years after the publication of *I Know Why the Caged Bird Sings*. Twenty-eight of these forty-four items have appeared since 1985, and only nine appeared before 1980 (and of these, two are interviews, one is bibliographic information, and one is a portion of a dissertation). There are different possibilities for interpreting these facts: on the one hand, it may be that scholarly critics have been slow to "catch up" to Angelou, slow to treat her work—and thus to recognize it—as literature worthy of their attention; on the other hand, it may be that the scholarly status of Angelou's work has risen in concert with poststructuralism's rise and has done so because poststructuralism has made it possible to appreciate Angelou's work in new ways.

3. For the significance of identity in *Caged Bird*, see Butterfield (203), Schmidt (25–27), McPherson (16, 18, 121), and Arensberg (275, 278–80, 288–90). On displacement, see Neubauer (117–19, 126–27) and Bloom (296–97). For a consideration of the personal vs. the universal, see McPherson (45–46), Cudjoe (10), O'Neale (26), McMurry (109), and Kinnamon, who stresses the importance of community in *Caged Bird* (123–33). On the "powhitetrash" scene, see Butterfield (210–12), McPherson (31–33), and McMurry (108). For an extensive consideration of the rape, see Froula (634–36). For the effect of the rape on Maya and her relationship with Mrs. Flowers, see Lionnet (147–52). For the graduation, see Butterfield (207), McMurry (109–10), Arensberg (283), and Cudjoe (14). For the visit to the

dentist, see Braxton (302–04) and Neubauer (118–19). For the month in the junkyard, see Gilbert (41) and Lionnet (156–57).

4. See Angelou's interviews with Tate ("Maya Angelou," 152) and with Neubauer ("Interview," 288–89). In an interview included in McPherson's *Order Out of Chaos*, Angelou mentions a number of incidents she omitted—some consciously, some unconsciously—from *Caged Bird* (138–40, 145–47, 157–58). O'Neale, who writes that Angelou's "narrative was held together by controlled techniques of artistic fiction" (26) and that her books are "arranged in loosely structured plot sequences which are skillfully controlled" (32), does not discuss these techniques or arrangements in any detail.

5. Angelou creates enough potential confusion about her protagonist's identity by having her called different names by different people—Ritie, Maya, Marguerite, Margaret, Mary, Sister. For the sake of consistency, I use the name "Maya" to refer to the protagonist of *Caged Bird* and the name "Angelou" to refer to its author.

7. Schmidt (25) and McPherson (26) comment on the episodic quality of *Caged Bird*. Schmidt is the one commentator on *Caged Bird* to mention that "each reminiscence forms a unit" (25). An indication of how episodic *Caged Bird* is is how readily selections from it have lent themselves to being anthologized.

LYMAN B. HAGEN ON BLACK MALE
AND FEMALE CHARACTERS IN THE BOOK

The title of Angelou's first long book, *I Know Why the Caged Bird Sings* (1970) . . . is taken from a line in Paul Laurence Dunbar's poem, "Sympathy." Asked by an interviewer why does the caged bird sing, Angelou replied,

> I think it was a bit of naivete or braggadocio . . . to say I know why the caged bird sings! I was copying a Paul Laurence Dunbar poem so it's all right. I believe that a free bird . . . floats down, eats the early worm, flies away, and mates. . . . But the bird that's in a cage stalks up and down, looking constantly out . . . and he sings about freedom. Mr. Paul Laurence Dunbar says,

I know why the caged bird sings, ah me, when his wing
is bruised and his bosom sore,—
When he beats his bars and he would be free;
It is not a carol of joy or glee,
But a prayer that he sends from his heart's deep core,
But a plea, that upward to Heaven he flings—
I know why the caged bird sings![1]

The book's title cleverly attracts readers while subtly reminding of the possibility of losing control or being denied freedom. Slaves and caged birds chirp their spirituals and flail against their constrictions. . . .

Transformation is the work's dominating theme, a metamorphosis of one who went from "being ignorant of being ignorant to being aware of being aware."[2] Throughout her writings, Angelou leaves a trail of overcoming parental and societal betrayal without espousing judgmental condemnations. Her maturation is shown by her responses to life's challenging situations. . . .

The stories, anecdotes, and jokes in *Caged Bird* do tell a dismaying story of white dominance, but *Caged Bird* in fact indicts nearly all of white society: American men, sheriffs, white con artists, white politicians, "crackers," uppity white women, white-trash children, all are targets. Their collective actions precipitate an outpouring of resentment from the African-American perspective. . . .

In Jungian archetypal terms, Angelou is the anima. The animus—the male part of her make-up—is represented by her brother Bailey. Bailey Johnson, Jr. is a firm, rather free-spirited youngster who because of being male, is able to move about in his segregated world with fewer restrictions than sister Maya. The two children are very close, probably because of their life situations as much as from their shared experiences and interests. They are both highly literate and adaptable. Bailey is protective of Maya, yet each appears to be very independent. Bailey must face greater dangers in the larger white-dominated world and is taught early on of the risks of being an African-American man. He does not allow this to prevent his functioning as a typical bright, energetic boy. He, more than any other character, with his outgoing personality and natural curiosity seems to exemplify Angelou's contention regarding blacks and whites: that they are more alike than unalike; that there are more similarities than differences. Bailey likes reading, comic books, movies, sportscasts, following around his St. Louis uncles and a little strutting. He idolizes his attractive, devil-may-care mother. All of these things could be said about any boy of his age. However, the promise of Bailey the boy seems to have been blunted for Bailey the man who wound up in prison. This is a sad, unfortunate development, but is not openly attributed to race. His embracing the street-style is accepted as a matter of circumstance and choice.

In addition to Bailey, whom the young Angelou acclaims the greatest person in her world, most male characters in *Caged Bird* receive exceptionally sympathetic treatment: there are the "dirt-disappointed" field workers, whose efforts weren't enough "no matter how much cotton they had picked" (*CB* 7); there is Daddy Clidell, a successful businessman; Grandfather Baxter, a family man of stature who had "mean" (tough) but not cruel sons; Uncle Willie, handicapped physically but not mentally; and Mr. McElroy who owned property. He was an "independent Black man, a near anachronism in Stamps" (*CB* 17). Even Mr. Freeman, the rapist of a child, had worldly status and held an important position with the railroad. In an interview with Claudia Tate Angelou said that she "wanted people to see that the man was not totally an ogre." These men all evidence strength and some attainment, even the worst of them. This would appear to be a conscious effort to minimize popular negative images of the African-American male.

Angelou's father, Bailey, Sr., does not fare so well. Here the personal outweighs the general. She confesses that "[her] father had not shown any particular pride in [her] and very little affection" (*CB* 195). Thus he is a "stranger" to her and someone to whom she did not feel any loyalty. His betrayal of the children was evidenced by his appearance in their lives only at times of moving them around—out of his way and responsibility. Her father lived in a fast lane characteristic of "hipster" types. In *Caged Bird* and in a later book, Angelou ridicules her father's speech habit of "er-er-ing" and his tendency to posture. Bailey, Sr. has all the earmarks of a blowhard. He wheels in and out of her early life with a lot of "pizazz," but little substance. He does not fill a major role, as a father should, but is seen more as a biological acknowledgment. Even he, however, survives and flourishes in his world, despite Angelou's low opinion of him. This lack of regard for Bailey, Sr. did not prevent Angelou from acknowledging the importance of a father figure to a family. Until her son is accepted as a grown man, she searches unsuccessfully for a man who would be a proper father and role model for him. She encounters only more betrayal.

Angelou's treatment of female role models in *Caged Bird*—of her Mrs. Flowers and of her mother and grandmothers—is even more positive than her treatment of African-American males. Since it is generally accepted that children of her era developed stronger bonds with their mother than their father, it is not surprising to find Angelou emphasizing the importance of mother and grandmothers. Such emphasis on mothers is, according to Stephanie A. Demetrakopoulos, "typical in women's autobiography due to the innate and archetypal aspects of the women's psyche, celebrated and codified long ago as the Eleusinian Mysteries."[24] These archetypal aspects may be incorporated in women's autobiographies, but it does not seem to be done consciously by Angelou. What she does do consciously, however, is to make an effort to counter unflattering female types described in the earlier literature by James Fenimore Cooper and Washington Irving. In this literature, grandmother matriarchs are depicted as silent, post-forty, corpulent and passively working in the kitchen.[25]

Compared to these earlier female stereotypes, Angelou's paternal grandmother, Mrs. Henderson, is a symbol of strength; she is in no way a weak, passive personality. She is not silent. She is the moral center and the voice of authority in *Caged Bird*. She is an Earth Mother, a figure who is good, kind, nurturing, and protecting. Angelou calls her "Momma" and in fiction she would be the "Madonna" figure, one who stands

85

for love and home. Her love for Angelou is unconditional and maternal. This love contrasts markedly with the paternal, in which love is more conditional and is usually earned and given only if one is obedient and attractive. In Angelou's extended family an atmosphere of warmth and love prevails that is not bestowed as a result of obedience or something earned. The strong maternal instinct enveloped all.

Momma Henderson, for all her matriarchal positioning, is a total realist. If she ever failed to do her duty or did not observe her place as a lower class citizen, she knows the white power structure would soon find a way to express its displeasure. Those in control are generally more interested in order than in justice. Momma's firm leadership while still being forced to keep her place, sends a mixed message to the younger generation that required a good deal of maturity and distancing for them to understand. It was some time before Angelou expressed, particularly in her poetry, the courage and patience of those who kept quiet and saw to the survival of those in whom the future rested.

Two other characteristics of Momma contrast with the matriarchs found in early American literature. Inasmuch as there were few or no opportunities in the professions, many women turned to religion as a means of escape from the confinement of their defined roles. Thus, Momma, a natural leader, became an important figure in her church. Moreover, Momma was an entrepreneur, a female rarity in the 1930s and unheard of one hundred years earlier. Her business acumen helped her family survive the depression and keep off relief; she preserved their independence. This would not be a role natural to her predecessors.

In addition to her praise of Momma Henderson, Angelou expresses great pride in her maternal grandmother, Mrs. Baxter, who did not take a back seat to anybody. As previously noted, she was very light-skinned and probably could have easily passed as white. She chose to remain a part of a black community. She and her family spoke standard English and provided important liaison with the local white power structure. She was a political activist who wielded considerable clout in her neighborhood in St. Louis, thus giving the lie to the myth that African Americans could not participate effectively in the political arena. Power blocks delivered votes and reaped the rewards. The Baxters understood the strength of unity. Similarly, Angelou's mother, Vivian Baxter Johnson, emerges as an extremely vital personality. She is Angelou's role model. Angelou absorbs her personal philosophy and frequently quotes her maxims of life. Mrs. Johnson's beauty and zest when she was young "made her powerful and her power made her unflinchingly honest" (*CB* 174); and "To describe (her) would be to write about a hurricane in its perfect power. Or the climbing, falling colors of a rainbow" (*CB* 49). Vivian is a city woman and sees no need in her world to conform to the subservient country folk tradition. She can sing and swing at will.

Vivian also found it too inconvenient to care for her two children or found it too incompatible with her life style. She finds an excuse—a depressed Maya—to send Maya and Bailey back to Stamps. This cavalier dumping of her children appears to Stephanie Demetrakopoulos as a failure to come to terms with the matriarchate (her mother), and this treatment, Demetrakopoulos finds, is a disturbing weakness of the book. Angelou's mother is seen as "shockingly callous" and insensitive by sending the little girl back to Stamps after being raped. Maya is traumatized by events and full of unwarranted guilt. The mother's behavior here and at other times does not justify the favorable treatment she got from Angelou and this action, Demetrakopoulos says, is "puzzling and unsettling.[26] Vivian is just as guilty as Bailey, Sr. of betraying their children. But Mother Vivian is idolized by both Johnson children and neither would dream of questioning her less-than-perfect mothering. She is all that is glamorous and movie-life desirable to them. . . .

Angelou['s] real purpose in *Caged Bird* . . . is to illuminate and explain her race's condition by protesting against white misconceptions and legitimizing the extremes sometimes required for survival. While justifying some questionable activities, she does not judge the right or wrong of them. She wants to destroy those stereotyped images of African Americans that prevailed when she wrote *Caged Bird*. Angelou rightly resents this thinking that dehumanized her people, and which continued to be practiced despite civil rights progress. Instead of writing an argumentative response or preaching to protest, Angelou chose the traditional form of autobiography to dramatize the conditions, presenting easily understood counter-examples. The reader can relate and conclude that the stereotype image is false and destructive. Forces beyond control dictate actions determined to be antisocial. Given equal opportunities, Angelou believes that like reactions would be demonstrated by blacks and whites.

Notes

1. Arthur E. Thomas, "Interview with Maya Angelou," *Like It Is: Arthur Thomas Interviews Leaders on Black America* (New York: Dutton, 1981), 6–7.

2. Maya Angelou, *I Know Why the Caged Bird Sings* (New York: Random House, 1970) 230. Hereafter cited in the text as *CB*.

24. Stephanie A. Demetrakopoulos, "The Metaphysics of Matrilinealism in Women's Autobiography," *Women's Autobiography: Essays in Criticism*, ed. Estelle C. Jelinek (Bloomington: Indiana University Press), 180–205.

25. Sandra O'Neale, "Reconstruction of the Composite Self: New Images of Black Women in Maya Angelou's Continuing Autobiography," *Black Women Writers 1950–1980*, ed. Mari Evans (New York: Anchor Books/Doubleday, 1984).

26. Demetrakopoulos 183.

MARION M. TANGUM AND MARJORIE SMELSTOR ON BEING CAUGHT IN THE GAZE

"Where is me? Ah don't see me."
—*Their Eyes Were Watching God*

"What you lookin' at me for?
I didn't come to stay. . . ."
—*I Know Why the Caged Bird Sings*

Integrating another fine art into a literary text, so that one artistic medium comments upon and provides an infrastructure for the literary, is, of course, a valued technique of American literature, particularly of African American literature. Slaves like Frederick Douglass who wrote narratives, as well as W. E. B. DuBois and Richard Wright, have all contributed to a rich tradition of the appropriation of other genres to create literary texts, a tradition that is legacy for other twentieth century writers to call upon.

Two of those more recent writers, Zora Neale Hurston and Maya Angelou, have built upon this tradition in a way that is new, creating verbal art that is thoroughly visual in technique. In two works of Hurston and Angelou, respectively, *Their Eyes Were Watching God* (1937) and *I Know Why the Caged Bird Sings* (1969), each of which has defied classification to any single genre, the constructs of visual art become sometimes the text's subject, sometimes its strategy, in ways that significantly alter the reader's participation in the text. We may question, as Janie does in our epigraph from *Their Eyes*, "Where is me? Ah don't see me" (21). The answer lies at times in the interconnectedness of reader, narrator, and character, through the intimacy of a beckoning, almost mesmerizing, "gaze," but then it lies in the position we assume as viewer, as subjects become distant—for viewing only: as the narratives compel us to remember, "What you lookin' at me for? I didn't come to stay."[1]

The ebb and flow of intersubjectivity that is at the center of *Their Eyes* and *Caged Bird* is created in both by a tension between, respectively, their author's artistic vision and their persona's or character's subjective "gaze." Through visual artistic techniques applied to language, Hurston and Angelou alternately hold the reader outside the text, offering a vision of aesthetics at work, and then, abruptly, through the starkly personal and riveting gaze of their characters or personae, compel the reader to enter—to experience personally—their works' reality. . . .

Margaret Olin's argument that two distinct arts, documentary and photography, become not only blurred but merged in *Let Us Now Praise Famous Men* (1941) provides the impetus for this study. In the case of its authors, James Agee and Walker Evans, merged genres result in a text that is transformed into a new type of art defined not by any similarities between the genres but, instead, by their differences: "When one regards the book as art, its documentary nature impertinently demands attention; but when regarded as documentary, its artistry intrudes" (92). Olin shows that Agee and Evans thus achieve a text that illuminates the "formative contradiction" of modern literature: the attempt to make of ostensibly hermetic art the engine of social change. Through the collaboration of camera and pen, Evans and Agee illuminate the reader's schizophrenic roles: as participant with the subjects, and therefore subjects themselves and, as spectator, able to appreciate a work of art that "presupposes distance and autonomy" (94). Authors, subjects, and readers are enmeshed in a web of intersubjectivity and then torn apart. But the aesthetic vision of the artists abruptly unravels that web, riveting our attention on the artistic object that has been created. The result, according to Olin, is a text that "repeatedly protests, down to its last sentence, that it is only about to begin" (112).

In the case of Hurston or Angelou, the result of this creation of schizophrenic roles for the reader is a tension between personally entering that realm and merely observing it, leading to a frustrating reading experience. . . .

From the first page of *Caged Bird*, too, Angelou offers a tantalizing invitation into her self—and then as promptly distances us from sharing that personal, all-of-a-sudden incommunicable, experience. This invitation to us to come in and gaze, then that sudden refusal to give us eye contact, is a process that recurs throughout the work. "What you looking at me for? I didn't come to stay . . ." (1). With these opening lines, the autobiography establishes a motif of gazing: willing members of the congregation of the Colored Methodist Episcopal Church, and readers who are willing, share a gaze with the young Angelou as she struggles to remember her memorized poem. Resembling the passages that appear in *Let Us Now Praise Famous Men* that Olin describes as incorporating three individuals—author, subject, reader—this direct invitation "takes the reader by the arm, exhorting 'you' to direct your gaze toward a photographed person" (105). But Olin warns that such an invitation is accepted at a price: "You are not going to be able to look 'this terrific thing in the eyes' unless you do so 'with all the summoning of heart you have'" (105). Gazing longer into the eyes of the child Angelou, as the author thrusts before us a repetition of the opening lines, we begin to grasp Olin's warning. Dolly McPherson has noted the importance of the opening lines in pointing to the importance of "something to look at" and has further suggested that since the persona is reciting an Easter poem, the "something to look at" is the persona as Christ (19). While the theme of cyclical renewal is present in the book, the prologue merely points to it. What the prologue actually augurs for and emphasizes is the suffering and descent preceding the rise and resurrection ultimately experienced by the maturing persona herself. And the narrative invites the reader to share this suffering and descent through sharing the gaze of the author and persona in the recreation of a poignant moment of childhood pain.

As the adult Angelou relates this experience, she acknowledges that her young self, a victim of "well-known forgetfulness" (1), had not forgotten the lines; instead, she had more important things to remember, which should be a cue that the opening of *Caged Bird* is more than the recreation pointed to above—that it will be a complexity created by a tension between narrator and subject, manifested by the tension between the vision of that adult and the gaze of the subject, the child.

Having been invited in to share the intensely personal gaze of young Maya, experiencing her pain with her as the shared gaze enables us to do, we participate in the text, in her embarrassment, in an entirely personal way. Prompted to recall her lines, young Maya becomes so flustered that she runs out of the church, tripping over a foot stuck out from the children's pew, and then suffers the unforgettable—which she relates to us by letting us gaze into her eyes so that we are present:

I stumbled and started to say something, or maybe to scream, but a green persimmon, or it could have been a lemon, caught me between the legs and squeezed....

Then, before I reached the door, the sting was burning down my legs and into my Sunday socks. I knew I'd have to let it go, or it would probably run right back up to my head and my poor head would burst like a dropped watermelon, and all my brains and spit and tongue and eyes would roll all over the place. (3)

But our gaze is abruptly interrupted: the narrative hand suddenly holds us at a distance, permitting us to view her plight objectively, not personally: "If growing up is painful for the Southern Black girl, being aware of her displacement is the rust on the razor that threatens the throat. It is an unnecessary insult" (1). First person becomes third; pronouns are almost entirely omitted. The metaphor of the rusty razor wrests our attention from the eyes and feelings of young Maya. Angelou seems to consciously grip the problem of modernism here: the potential to lose ourselves in the mesmerizing gaze of the subject and so become subjects ourselves, inaccessible to the artistic vision competing with that compelling gaze. She commandingly pulls us back to observe from a distance, shifting her tense and forcing us to shift our viewing perspective, away from a familiar and thus comforting place in Angelou's and our own pasts into a discomforting, disconcerting present that makes indirect object of what had been subject, grammatically separating us from the southern black girl and so insuring that we can "see" her. Our, Maya's and our, personal recollection of that morning at the Colored Methodist Episcopal Church yields to the reality of victimization and its social consequences—and an appreciation of the art of the metaphor and the power of language, without which we remain subject and only subject. The gaze that reverts to the vision, through the alterations of language alone, makes problematic, and so keeps supple, the position of the audience in *Caged Bird*.

Notes
1. By gaze, we do not mean the penetrating, degenerating probe of a seer on the seen, which feminist critics have rightly identified as

the means of objectification of the person being viewed. Rather, we use the term as Margaret Olin does in her article on the "Privilege of Perception" which we discuss further on.

SIPHOKAZI KOYANA AND ROSEMARY GRAY ON ANGELOU'S SELF-EMPOWERMENT

A comparison between Angelou's *I Know Why the Caged Bird Sings* (1969) and Magona's *To My Children's Children* (1990) reveals that the characters' journeys from childhood to untimely young motherhood have much in common, but ultimately bear an inverse relationship to each other. Their emerging sense of female selfhood is especially linked to cultural issues as well as the political structures in the USA and South Africa during the 1940s and 50s: namely civil rights, on the one hand, and apartheid, on the other. Broadly speaking, [Maya] Angelou moves from anxious toddler to confident teenager, whereas [Sindiwe] Magona regresses from secure childhood to anxious youngster. Paradoxically, although black South Africans had a culture of their own, they had fewer opportunities in the dominant culture. By contrast, African-Americans (as a group) had, and have, greater access to active roles even though they are more dependent on the dominant culture. Not unnaturally, the extent of each group's access to opportunities depends on the constitutional rights or restrictions in each country, as is reflected, for example, in the elimination of school segregation in the United States (Brown vs. Board of Education of Topeka, 1954) at the time that it was enforced in South Africa (Bantu Education Act, 1955).

This distinction between the progressive American schooling system and the repressive South African one has a significant impact on the two young lives, producing an emergent consciousness of empowerment versus powerlessness; integration versus isolation; and identification or acculturation versus alienation. . . .

Angelou's childhood consciousness is . . . conditioned by the sense of otherness [and] more authentically childlike, generated as it is by her excruciating sense of her own ugliness simply because she is not white. This emanates from her awareness of her physical dissimilarity to the doll-like, blond, white child-icon Shirley Temple. Her negative self-image is so strong that she imagines her misfortune of being born black (in 1928) as a "black ugly dream" from which she hopes one day to awake (*Caged Bird* 2). This negativity is intensified by parental rejection: at three, she is packed off with her four-year-old brother to Arkansas by incompatible parents. Her sense of loss and emotional displacement, common among children of parents undergoing divorce, is amplified not only by the geographical relocation by train but also by the fact that neither of the parents communicates with the children for the next three years.

However, there are two 'pillars' on which Maya leans in these lonely early years: the unwavering protection of Momma (Maya's paternal grandmother and the only black storekeeper and property owner in Stamps) and the companionship of her brother, Bailey. Momma, whose world is "bordered on all sides with work, duty, religion and 'her place'" (57), provides her granddaughter with stability and a positive model of black female empowerment. As an active and devout member of her church, Momma introduces Maya to Christianity and its values as a mechanism for spiritual survival and political advancement, a role religion has played throughout the history of blacks in America.[3]

In contrast to the disruption of Christianity in Sindiwe's traditional religion [. . .]), Christianity is liberating for Maya. The church is one of the few institutions where the black community can congregate without fear. In short, the role that Momma plays in anchoring Maya's life attests to both the strength of belief (faith) and black solidarity. Even though economic displacement often compels biological parents to live without their children, in America as in South Africa, "the grandmother can be counted upon to provide physical protection and spiritual nourishment, to perpetuate family history, and to retain and transmit moral values for the children" (Hill-Lubin 258). These strong bonds of the extended family as well as the adaptability of family roles within such structures are among the characteristics that have fostered the survival of black families and bereft individuals within those families. . . .

Maya's inability to respond to her mother emotionally, when she finally moves in with Vivian, is one of the saddest features of her childhood. Assailed by this stranger's beauty, the child handles this estrangement by turning inward, blaming her own imagined 'handicap.' In her eyes she lacks the beauty that she, her mother, and American society value so highly.[6] Maya's only solace is her mother's beauty, although this is poor consolation for an absence of maternal affection. Yet, it is precisely this reluctance to reject, judge, or condemn Vivian's violent, fast-paced, daredevil lifestyle that facilitates their later reconciliation after Maya produces a son.

This reconciliation is surprising and even ironic as the decisive trauma in the eight-year-old Maya's life was rape by Mr Freeman, Vivian's live-in boyfriend. Rape underscores both the helplessness of children and the gendered nature of that helplessness. As a girl child, Maya is much more vulnerable to sexual molestation than her brother. The enormity of the trauma, perpetrated by one she had looked upon as a father figure, coupled with the pain of penetration, threats of violence and the rapist's subsequent death, not surprisingly prove more than Maya can handle; and six bleak years of autistic muteness follow.

Because the black child is burdened by the cultural and domestic conspiracy of silence in matters regarding the sexual violation of juveniles, it was to be decades before Angelou could disclose in writing the pain she experienced in this episode. Nevertheless, her honest portrayal of the rape (her sensitivity to the victim at a time when rape victims were generally believed to have seduced their attackers), and her political decision to expose how black males, in the cruellest game of power, violate black females as if they were mere ciphers, making even heavier the crosses they bear, emphasise her courage and initiative as a writer. Angelou poignantly portrays the victim's psychological landscape: first, her need for parental love and intimacy, and later, her confusion, guilt and fear. Even more importantly, Angelou's testimony challenges the practice of suppressing gender in the name of broader racial concerns, as was the case in both the Civil Rights and the Black Power Movements. . . .

In the United States race and sex have always been overlapping discourses, a fact that has its origins in slavery.[7] Angelou asserts that the profound impact of rape is best understood in the context of rape as a crime against the person and not the hymen. She correctly depicts rape as a political act by which men attempt to assert their domination over women.

Such effective use of autobiography in consciousness-raising broke what, in retrospect, seems a remarkable silence about a pervasive aspect of the young female experience. It also effectively led to subsequent strategies for change, ranging from feminist self-help methods of rape crisis centres to reform of the criminal justice and medical care systems.[8] . . .

[The] major setbacks in the young Maya's life are counterbalanced by her scholastic aptitude, encouragement by her teachers, drama and dance classes, culminating in a role in the musical "Porgy and Bess" as a singular achievement in Maya's career in theatre. Reading provides the first step out of the pit of despair. Back in Stamps after the rape, Maya is helped by Momma's friend, Mrs Flowers, to regain her speech through reciting the poetry she loves so much. Later, in San Francisco, her class teacher, Miss Kirwin, stimulates her intellectually by challenging her to learn about current affairs; while her extracurricular dance and drama classes teach Maya to be less self-conscious. Repeatedly tossed between city and rural life, Maya learns to identify with both localities. She takes shelter in the "soft breath of anonymity" (*Caged Bird* 212) that shrouds and cushions her bashful self in San Francisco's "air of collective displacement, the impermanence of life in wartime" (211) as surely as she rebuilds her cocoon in the social devastation and barren nothingness of Stamps. Thus Maya creatively reconstitutes the physical landscape as the contestatory site of a decentred subject-in-progress whose homecoming entails painful border crossings.

Particular incidents that Angelou stresses as triumphs in her adolescence are her adventure in Mexico, her stay in the junkyard, and her successful struggle for employment in the railways. The trip to Mexico involves Maya's manoeuvre of her drunken father's car down a treacherous mountain at night. The thrill that she feels after this daring success awakens her potential to control her own destiny.

The second incident results in the acquisition of even greater confidence for she manages to survive a month in a junkyard after being stabbed by her father's girlfriend.[9] Here, the unquestioning acceptance by her displaced peers enables her to find acceptance as an equal in a peaceful, multi-racial community, an experience that also marks the beginnings of racial tolerance in Maya's life. Moreover, the lack of criticism strengthens her ego and makes Maya realise her potential to survive, even without adult support.

The third empowering incident is Maya's relentless determination to challenge the San Francisco Rail company to employ her as its first black streetcar 'conductorette,' which demonstrates the strength of her growing self-esteem. Having taken a semester off from school to work after her sixteen-year-old brother leaves home, Maya finally gets the job she wants and enjoys, at a time when many older black women still endured the drudgery of either domestic and janitorial work or low-level clerkship. This last episode has the benefit of improving Maya's relations with her mother (Vivian is impressed by her daughter's efforts to challenge racism independently); and Suzette Henke pertinently asks: "If discrimination can be overcome by the patient self-assertion of a lone, determined teenager, what might racial solidarity and communal black struggle for empowerment not achieve?" (213).

Although still young, Maya thus demonstrates the potential for agency precisely because, ironically, she is and always has been so enmeshed in the everyday struggles of black people. Her ability to become the first black 'conductorette,' therefore, affirms resources for resistance and hope instead of always showing blacks as victims of oppression in a manner that reproduces the punitive power it critiques. In time, Maya's work success as employee, performer, and writer leads her into the political arena and work with Dr Martin Luther King in the Civil Rights Movement.

Notes

3. In the times of slavery, religion served as a stimulant for the many rebellions that took place. Escaping to Canada was often seen as a journey towards Canaan, comparable to that of the Biblical Israelites escaping from Egypt. Religion was also a major source of strength during the Civil Rights Movement of the 1950s and 60s, with Dr Martin Luther King, like Harriet Tubman generations before, symbolising Moses' guidance towards the Promised Land.

6. Lynn Bloom (294) also observes that instead of blaming her mother for not being the ideal, nurturing, maternal figure, Maya blames her own imagined deficiencies for the detachment.

7. Dating back to slavery when white men maintained their political and economic power by raping black women as a right and a rite, black men felt emasculated as they could neither protect nor control their own women. Rape was, therefore, a form of symbolic castration. Consequently, the black man defined his attempt to control (and abuse) black women as reclaiming his lost manhood. For further analysis of this issue, see Hooks (57–64).

8. Angelou registers the insensitivity of the health care staff by showing how instead of sympathising with her, the nurses tell her that she no longer has anything to fear: the worst is over for her. Similarly, Angelou portrays the rape victim's unenviable position in the courtroom in which Mr Freeman's lawyer ridicules her for not knowing what the rapist was wearing when he raped her.

9. After her father's insecure live-in girlfriend stabs her in the abdomen with a knife during a fight, Maya runs away to a junkyard where she stays until the wound heals. Maya fears Vivian will retaliate if she finds out that her daughter has been wounded.

YOLANDA PIERCE ON RESILIENCE AND BLACK MOTHERHOOD

As the first volume of a five-volume autobiographical series, Maya Angelou's *I Know Why the Caged Bird Sings* is the triumphant account of several Black women raising a young Black girl in a racist and sexist society. This book reveals how Black women love themselves and each other despite living in a world that does not love or value them. Angelou's autobiography describes a collective identity of Black women who support each other and still remain individuals, free to sing their own songs of freedom.

Angelou writes: "if growing up is painful for the Southern black girl, being aware of her displacement is the rust on the razor that threatens the throat. It is an unnecessary insult" (4). Her autobiography deals with the painful double strikes of growing up Black and female. As a young girl, Marguerite Johnson longs to be white, to be a member of what she perceives as the more favored race. She wants to wake up out of her "ugly black dream" and instead find herself with long blond hair and blue eyes (2). She understands, even as a little girl, that her "nappy black hair" and dark skin are not prized. She begins her life with the pain of not being "good enough," since she could not find girls who looked like her in any books or movies.

Marguerite experiences the pain of racism as she watches her beloved paternal grandmother endure humiliation when white girls call her "Annie" instead of respectfully addressing her as "Mrs. Henderson." As a teenager, Marguerite has a similar experience in which she is "called out of her name" by a white female employer who attempts to rename her "Mary" (108). Momma Henderson's bitter experiences have prepared Marguerite for her own confrontations with racist America. The refusal of a white dentist, to whom Momma Henderson has lent money, to perform badly needed dental work on Marguerite is another example of the humiliation these two generations of Black women face together. Told by the dentist that he would "rather stick [his] hand in a dog's mouth than in a nigger's," granddaughter and grandmother are forced to travel twenty-five miles to the nearest Black dentist (189). The repercussions of Jim Crow, even eighty years after slavery, place Black women at the very bottom of a white patriarchal system.

And yet despite the pain and humiliations of racism, Angelou's autobiography is a tale of triumph and a celebration of the strength of Black womanhood. Momma Henderson is a strong, self-made, economically independent woman who has learned to operate and succeed in a world that believes women should be submissive and dependent. Despite demeaning confrontations with those who attempt to humiliate her, Momma Henderson is always the victor because she never relinquishes her self-respect—and she teaches Marguerite to do the same. Likewise, her maternal grandmother, "Grandmother Baxter" raises her "six mean children" in an effort to prepare them to deal with a mean world (62). It is she who is responsible for punishing Mr. Freeman after he rapes 8-year-old Marguerite. Knowing that the legal system often does not protect Black people, Grandmother Baxter takes the law into her own hands.

Vivian Baxter, Marguerite's mother, is a woman of great resourcefulness, like her own mother. She takes joy and pleasure out of life, despite life's pains. From her, Marguerite learns the joys of being a woman, delighting in the feminine, and being proud of her Black body. Mrs. Flowers, the "aristocrat" of Stamps, Arkansas, also encourages Marguerite to be "proud to be a Negro" (95). She helps Marguerite regain her voice after the rape; she teaches her about the importance of language; she exposes her to great literature; and she gives her "lessons in living" so that Marguerite would learn to listen "carefully to what country people called mother wit . . . couched in the collective wisdom of generations" (100). All of these women teach Marguerite to love herself, and to love the generations of Black women who have come before her and helped pave a road of freedom in a restrictive world.

At sixteen, Marguerite becomes the first African-American street car conductor, due in large part to the tenacity that her mothers, grandmothers, and "other mothers" have taught her. At the end of her autobiography, Marguerite herself becomes a mother, and in that role she has to draw upon all the collective wisdom taught to her. Angelou writes that Black women are often "assaulted in [their] tender years" by male dominance, white hatred, and powerlessness, so the fact that adult Black women survive and emerge as formidable human beings is deserving of respect (272). Feminist historian Elizabeth Fox-Genovese echoes these sentiments, suggesting that Angelou deliberately "links herself to the Southern roots and history of her people" and to those "American Negro female survivors whom she implicitly credits with laying the foundation for her own survival" (23).

Students should pay particular attention to the themes and definitions of motherhood within this book; an important exercise would be to list the multiple "other mothers" and discuss why Black motherhood is not dependent on the presence of an actual biological mother. Students must also examine self-definition as a continuous theme in *I Know Why the Caged Bird Sings*; and central to the text is Angelou's search for a place in which both blackness and womanhood can be celebrated.

Finally, despite its controversy, neither students nor teachers should be intimidated by the sexual content of Angelou's autobiography. What makes her work particularly powerful is her discussion of the vulnerable sexual positions in which all girls and women are placed. As the issue of childhood sexual abuse continues to be silenced within our society, Angelou's autobiography is a starting point in shattering that silence and finding a place of healing.

Works by Maya Angelou

I Know Why the Caged Bird Sings, 1970.

Just Give Me a Cool Drink of Water 'fore I Diiie, 1971.

Gather Together in My Name, 1974.

Oh Pray My Wings Are Gonna Fit Me Well, 1975.

Singin' and Swingin' and Gettin' Merry Like Christmas, 1976.

And Still I Rise, 1978.

The Heart of a Woman, 1981.

Shaker, Why Don't You Sing?, 1983.

All God's Children Need Traveling Shoes, 1986.

Mrs. Flowers: A Moment of Friendship, 1986.

Poems: Maya Angelou, 1986.

Now Sheba Sings the Song, 1987.

I Shall Not Be Moved, 1990.

Wouldn't Take Nothing for My Journey Now, 1993.

Soul Looks Back in Wonder, 1993.

Life Doesn't Frighten Me, 1993.

On the Pulse of Morning, 1993.

The Complete Collected Poems of Maya Angelou, 1994.

My Painted House, My Friendly Chicken, and Me, 1994.

Phenomenal Woman: Four Poems Celebrating Women, 1995.

A Brave and Startling Truth, 1995.

Kofi and His Magic, 1996.

Even the Stars Look Lonesome, 1997.

A Song Flung Up to Heaven, 2002.

Annotated Bibliography

Arensberg, Liliane K., "Death as a Metaphor of Self in *I Know Why the Caged Bird Sings*," *CLA Journal* 20, no. 2 (December 1976).

Noting that Angelou's work can be understood as a "personal confession of racial self-hatred," Arensberg argues that Angelou's motivation was less driven by a need to fit in and more fueled by a need to distinguish herself.

Braxton, Joanne M. *Maya Angelou's "I Know Why the Caged Bird Sings": A Casebook.* New York and Oxford: Oxford University Press, 1999.

This volume from the Casebook series presents nine essays about the author and her debut work. Beginning and ending this study are two essays that incorporate Angelou's own words: the first by editor Joanne M. Braxton, who introduces the author to the reader and incorporates part of a conversation the women had, and the second offered by Claudia Tate from an interview she had with the author in 1983. Among the most interesting of these essays is one by Opal Moore, who examines the history of censorship related to *Caged Bird* and speculates about the complaints raised and the compelling reasons such censorship deprives students of a chance to discuss issues critical in their lives.

Cudjoe, Selwyn R. "Maya Angelou: The Autobiographical Statement Updated." From *Reading Black, Reading Feminist: A Critical Anthology.* Henry Louis Gates Jr., ed. New York: Meridian, 1990.

Cudjoe reads in Angelou's first work an attempt to illuminate the sins and failings of all people, not merely a diatribe against the destructive menace of white racism.

Fisher, Jerilyn and Ellen S. Silber, eds. *Women in Literature: Reading through the Lens of Gender.* Westport, Connecticut and London: Greenwood Press, 2003.

This volume consists of dozens of essays by different writers on the presence and influence of women in classical and contemporary literature. The essay by Yolanda Pierce on *Caged Bird* appears in this comprehensive study.

Froula, Christine. "The Daughter's Seduction: Sexual Violence and Literary History," *Signs* 11, no. 4 (Summer 1986): 621–644.

Froula explores what she sees as the limits imposed, from Homer through Sigmund Freud, on male and female to silence women's speech when it threatens a father's power. Froula shows how *I Know Why the Caged Bird Sings* and *The Color Purple* resist this convention.

Gilbert, Susan. "Maya Angelou's *I Know Why the Caged Bird Sings:* Paths to Escape." From *Mount Olive Review* 1, no. 1 Spring 1987, pp. 39–50, and *"Maya Angelou's "I Know Why the Caged Bird Sings": A Casebook.* New York and Oxford: Oxford University Press, 1999: 99–110.

Gilbert writes persuasively and admiringly of Maya Angelou as a writer and woman who has not held herself back by remaining preoccupied with exclusively southern and provincial issues.

Hagen, Lyman B. *Heart of a Woman, Mind of a Writer, and Soul of a Poet: A Critical Analysis of the Writings of Maya Angelou.* Lanham, MD; New York; and London: University Press of New England, 1997.

This volume attempts to introduce Maya Angelou's life and work to new audiences. It begins with a chapter discussing Angelou's distinctive blend of autobiographical and narrative writing. A second chapter offers a selective and nonchronological biography emphasizing the personal strengths and the appalling destructivity of racism that characterized Angelou's years of growing up. Five of Angelou's personal narratives (the autobiographies) are discussed in sequence in the next chapter. Some young readers may not know about Angelou's poetry career that culminated in her recitation of a poem requested by President Clinton for his inauguration ceremony. This poem (which Angelou thought appropriate for the occasion but not otherwise a "great" poem) and others are discussed in the fourth chapter. Angelou has earned public recognition, and her more public engagements and activities are discussed in the fifth chapter. Chapter 6 deals with the history and explanations generated by the banning in some school communities of *I Know Why the Caged Bird Sings* and *Gather Together in My Name*. In the final chapter, the author comments on Angelou's public presence and impact.

Kinnamon, Keneth. "Call and Response: Intertextuality in Two Autobiographical Works by Richard Wright and Maya Angelou." In *Studies in Black American Literature, Vol. II: Belief vs. Theory in Black American Literary Criticism*. Ed. William L. Andrews, 121–134. Greenwood, Fla: Penkevill Publishing, 1986.

Kinnamon expands on Robert B. Stepto's study of black American male writers in their search for freedom and education. Kinnamon compares Angelou's *I Know Why the Caged Bird Sings* to Richard Wright's *Black Boy* and looks at how their views may be different because of the authors' genders. He also explores the focus on community in both books.

Lionnet, Françoise. "Con Artists and Storytellers: Maya Angelou's Problematic Sense of Audience." In *Autobiographical Voices: Race, Gender, Self-Portraiture*. Ithaca, N.Y.: Cornell University Press, 1989, 130–166.

While other critics have commented on the fact that autobiography is not necessarily truth, Lionnet explains in detail that Angelou is torn, struggling in her quest to write for both white and black audiences. Lionnet explores Angelou's technique in terms of the narrator's own love of literature, her use of religion, and her experience with various methods of communication deriving from folk traditions.

Lupton, Mary Jane. "Singing the Black Mother: Maya Angelou and Autobiographical Continuity," *Black American Literature Forum* 24, no. 2 (Summer 1990): 257–276.

Lupton concentrates on motherhood and the relationship between mother and child as a unifier within *I Know Why the Caged Bird Sings*, within Angelou's other biographies, and connecting the series of works to one another. She contends the autobiographical works are also connected by a focus on creative work and motherhood.

O'Neale, Sondra. "Reconstruction of the Composite Self: New Images of Black Women in Maya Angelou's Continuing Autobiography." In *Black Women Writers (1950–1980), A Critical Evaluation*. Ed. Mari Evans. Garden City, N.Y.: Doubleday, 1984: 25–36.

O'Neale remarks that, whereas there have been stereotyped visions of black women in literature, in *I Know Why the Caged Bird Sings*, Angelou presents a revised view, a composite she draws from the strong women in her book as well as from black history. Additionally, O'Neale examines how Angelou's self develops from knowledge gained through art and literature and how Angelou realizes that to control her life she must rely on her own powerful intellect.

Saunders, James Robert. "Breaking Out of the Cage: The Autobiographical Writings of Maya Angelou," *The Hollins Critic* 28, no. 4 (October 1991): 1–11.

Saunders reevaluates Stephen Butterfield's view of *I Know Why the Caged Bird Sings*, in what Saunders calls Butterfield's "seminal work," *Black Autobiography in America*. Saunders agrees that *Caged Bird* fits in with the slave narrative tradition, due especially to its focus on the importance of education, even for those in terrible circumstances. He disagrees with Butterfield, though, in terms of when confidence is truly attained in Angelou's work.

Tangum, Marion M., and Marjorie Smelstor. "Hurston's and Angelou's Visual Art: The Distancing Vision and the Beckoning Gaze," from *The Southern Literary Journal* 31, no.1 (Fall 1998): 80–97.

The authors present an interesting comparison of the methods used by both Hurston and Angelou to create dual perspectives within their works—namely, the story told in the perspective of the author as she is herself experiencing it and the perspective of the author as she is looking back on the episode and commenting on it. The reader experiences a confusion of place and perspective.

Vermillion, Mary. "Reembodying the Self: Representations of Rape in *Incidents in the Life of a Slave Girl* and *I Know Why the Caged Bird Sings,*" *Biography* 15, no. 3 (Summer 1992): 243–260.

While other critics have commented on the way Angelou portrays and presents the rape in *I Know Why the Caged Bird Sings*, Vermillion examines it in terms of its historical context as well by comparing Angelou's book with the antebellum autobiography *Incidents in the Life of a Slave Girl*. Vermillion carefully observes how in both books the authors "reembody" the raped women. She pays careful attention to Angelou's foreshadowing and language.

Walker, Pierre A. "Racial Protest, Identity, Words, and Form in Maya Angelou's *I Know Why the Caged Bird Sings,*" *College Literature* 22, no. 3 (October 1995): 91–108.

Walker looks at *I Know Why the Caged Bird Sings* in the African-American literary tradition but focuses on Angelou's political message and accomplishment in the book. He points in detail to Angelou's strength in juxtaposing chapters, in having groups of chapters show a progression of theme, and in carefully orchestrating each chapter's design.

Contributors

Harold Bloom is Sterling Professor of the Humanities at Yale University. Educated at Cornell and Yale universities, he is the author of more than 30 books, including *Shelley's Mythmaking* (1959), *The Visionary Company* (1961), *Blake's Apocalypse* (1963), *Yeats* (1970), *The Anxiety of Influence* (1973), *A Map of Misreading* (1975), *Kabbalah and Criticism* (1975), *Agon: Toward a Theory of Revisionism* (1982), *The American Religion* (1992), *The Western Canon* (1994), *Omens of Millennium: The Gnosis of Angels, Dreams, and Resurrection* (1996), *Shakespeare: The Invention of the Human* (1998), *How to Read and Why* (2000), *Genius: A Mosaic of One Hundred Exemplary Creative Minds* (2002), *Hamlet: Poem Unlimited* (2003), *Where Shall Wisdom Be Found?* (2004), and *Jesus and Yahweh: The Names Divine* (2005). In addition, he is the author of hundreds of articles, reviews, and editorial introductions. In 1999, Professor Bloom received the American Academy of Arts and Letters' Gold Medal for Criticism. He has also received the International Prize of Catalonia, the Alfonso Reyes Prize of Mexico, and the Hans Christian Andersen Bicentennial Prize of Denmark.

Liliane K. Arensberg has contributed essays to *American Notes & Queries*.

Susan Gilbert is the author of "Maya Angelou's *I Know Why the Caged Bird Sings:* Paths to Escape" and has contributed to *Maya Angelou's "I Know Why the Caged Bird Sings": A Casebook*.

Carol E. Neubauer teaches English and foreign languages at Bradley University. She has also written about the life and work of Maxine Hong Kingston.

Elizabeth Fox-Genovese was, before her death in 2007, a tenured professor at Emory University. She founded and directed the university's Institute for Women's Studies. In addition to her work on Maya Angelou, Fox-Genovese was the author of *Within the Plantation Household: Black and White Women of the Old South* (1988); *To Be Worthy of God's Favor: Southern Women's Defense and Critique of Slavery* (1993); and, with her husband, Eugene Genovese, *The Mind of the Master Class: History and Faith in the Southern Slaveholders* (2005).

Onita Estes-Hicks is chairwoman of the English Language Studies Program at SUNY, Old Westbury. Currently, she is planning a study of the work of writer Jean Toomer.

Opal Moore is a poet, essayist, and writer of short stories whose earliest influences were the works of Toni Morrison and Gwendolyn Brooks. She is chairwoman of the English department at Spelman College. In 2004, she published *Lot's Daughters*.

Pierre A. Walker has served as assistant professor of English at Western Michigan University.

Lyman B. Hagen has been affiliated with Arkansas State University and the Arkansas Endowment for the Humanities.

Marion M. Tangum has also written commentary about Larry McMurtry's novel *Lonesome Dove*. Tangum is associated with Southwest Texas State University and has participated as a presenter in the Rocky Mountain Modern Language Association Convention in 2003.

Marjorie Smelstor is co-author of the essay "Hurston's and Angelou's Visual Art: The Distancing Vision and the Beckoning Gaze."

Siphokazi Koyana is a research fellow in English at the University of Pretoria, focusing on the work of black South African and African-American women writers.

Rosemary Gray teaches in the English department at the University of Pretoria, where she is also head of research and president of the English Academy. Her research focus has been writers of African literature.

Yolanda Pierce has been an assistant professor of English and African-American studies at the University of Kentucky. Her research interests are American slave narratives, African-American autobiography, the black church tradition, and black women writers.

Acknowledgments

Liliane K. Arensberg, excerpts of "Death as Metaphor of Self in *I Know Why the Caged Bird Sings*." From *College Language Association Journal* 20, no. 2 (December 1976): 273–91. Copyright © 1976 *CLA Journal*.

Susan Gilbert, excerpts of "Maya Angelou's *I Know Why the Caged Bird Sings*: Paths to Escape." From *Mount Olive Review* 1, no. 1 (Spring 1987): 39–50. Copyright © 1987 Mount Olive College Press.

Carol E. Neubauer, "An Interview with Maya Angelou." From *The Massachusetts Review* 28, no. 2 (Summer 1987): 286–92. Copyright © 1987 *The Massachusetts Review*.

Elizabeth Fox-Genovese, "Myth and History: Discourse of Origins in Zora Neale Hurston and Maya Angelou." From *Black American Literature Forum* 24, no. 2 (Summer 1990): 221–36. Copyright © 1990 the estate of Elizabeth Fox-Genovese.

Onita Estes-Hicks, "The Way We Were: Precious Memories of the Black Segregated South." From *African American Review* 27, no. 1 (Spring 1993): 9–19. Copyright © 1993 by Onita Estes-Hicks.

Opal Moore, "Learning to Live: When the Bird Breaks from the Cage." From *Censored Books: Critical Viewpoints,* edited by Nicholas J. Karolides, Lee Burress, and John M. Kean. Published by Metuchen Press. Copyright © 1993 by Opal Moore.

Pierre A. Walker, "Racial Protest, Identity, Words, and Form in Maya Angelou's *I Know Why the Caged Bird Sings*." From *College Literature* 22, no. 3 (October 1995): 91–108. Copyright © 1995 *College Literature*.

Index

Characters in literary works are indexed by first name (if any), followed by the name of the work in parentheses.